# LEVEL 1

# SAFE
## ROAD SKILLS
## AND ATTITUDES

Andy Ashton

ALWAYS LEARNING

**PEARSON**

Published by Pearson Education Limited, Edinburgh Gate, Harlow, Essex, CM20 2JE.

www.pearsonschoolsandfecolleges.co.uk

Text © Andy Ashton, 2012
Designed by Wooden Ark (Leeds)
Typeset by Tek-Art, Crawley Down, West Sussex
Original illustrations © Pearson Education Ltd, 2012
Illustrated by Stephanie Strickland
Cover design by Wooden Ark (Leeds)
Picture research by Chrissie Martin
Cover photo © DSA/Crown copyright

The right of Andy Ashton to be identified as author of this work has been asserted by him in accordance with the Copyright, Designs and Patents Act 1988.

First published 2012

16 15 14 13 12
10 9 8 7 6 5 4 3 2 1

**British Library Cataloguing in Publication Data**
A catalogue record for this book is available from the British Library

ISBN 978 1 408272 01 5

Printed in the UK by Scotprint

**Disclaimer**
This material has been published on behalf of Edexcel and offers high-quality support for the delivery of Edexcel qualifications.

This does not mean that the material is essential to achieve any Edexcel qualification, nor does it mean that it is the only suitable material available to support any Edexcel qualification. Material from this publication will not be used verbatim in any examination or assessment set by Edexcel. Any resource lists produced by Edexcel shall include this and other appropriate resources.

Copies of official specifications for all Edexcel qualifications may be found on the Edexcel website: www.edexcel.com

# Contents

Acknowledgements iv

Introduction v

**Unit 1:** Preparing for a safe journey by road 1

**Unit 2:** Maintaining own and others' safety in relation to vehicles 23

**Unit 3:** Knowing the rules of the road 49

**Unit 4:** Recognising safe road use 75

Index 101

# Acknowledgements

The author and publisher would like to thank the following individuals and organisations for permission to reproduce photographs:

(Key: b-bottom; c-centre; l-left; r-right; t-top)

**Alamy Images:** Ashley Cooper Pics 56, by Ian Miles - Flashpoint Pictures 51, Carol Bond 8, Christina Kennedy 85, Jupiter Images / Brand X 16, Justin Kase 78, Mark Richardson 71, Motoring Picture Library 3, Photo Cornwell 80; **DSA / Crown Copyright:** 1, 18, 20, 29, 32, 34, 40, 49, 54, 55, 58, 61, 73, 88, 91; **Imagestate Media:** John Foxx Collection 14, Michael Duerindex 4; **Masterfile UK Ltd:** 75; **Pearson Education Ltd:** Mark Bassett 50; **Shutterstock.com:** fotosub 35, imageegami 46, Mohd Nor Azim Bin Ridzuan 97; **www.imagesource.com:** 23

All other images © Pearson Education

Every effort has been made to contact copyright holders of material reproduced in this book. Any omissions will be rectified in subsequent printings if notice is given to the publishers.

Peason Education would like to thank the DSA for their support in providing photos and reviewing text for this publication.

## Author acknowledgements

Andy Ashton would like to thank all the people who have supported him during the writing period. These include 'the usual suspects' and Steve K, Dan R, Cheryl S and Steve S for their specialist input and advice.

This book is dedicated to all those people who have been affected in any way by road traffic accidents.

# Introduction

This book has been written to help you achieve either the Award or Certificate in Safe Road Skills and Attitudes. It will also help you to develop the background knowledge and skills you need to be effective and considerate road users.

# What will I learn, and how will I be assessed, during the course?

## Certificate

The certificate course is divided into 4 units:

**Unit 1** aims to help you understand how to prepare for a safe journey by road. You will develop an understanding of the costs and benefits of different forms of transport and consider different methods of planning a journey, such as map reading and the use of satellite navigation. You will then plan a journey using map-reading skills. At the end of this unit, you will produce a portfolio of evidence to meet the assessment criteria.

**Unit 2** will help you to understand the regular checks that need to be carried out on different forms of transport, such as cars or bicycles. You will need to complete these checks and present evidence to support this in your portfolio. This unit also requires you to develop your knowledge and understanding of how to respond in cases of breakdown or accident. At the end of this unit, you will produce a portfolio of evidence to meet the assessment criteria.

**Unit 3** will develop your understanding of some of the rules of the road. You will also consider how vulnerable road users can stay safe when using the roads and how to stay safe at level crossings and tramways. This unit also requires an understanding of the Highway Code rules that relate to signs and signals. This unit is assessed by an online multiple-choice test that is externally set and marked by Edexcel. There are 20 items and learners must achieve 17 to pass.

**Unit 4** combines some of the content from other units. You will develop an understanding of the different types of vulnerable road users and how different methods of traffic calming can improve general road safety. In the last part of this unit, you will develop your knowledge about how the behaviours and attitudes of road users, such as 'road rage' or 'failure to show consideration for others' can affect the safety of others. At the end of this unit, you will produce a portfolio of evidence to meet the assessment criteria.

## Certificate

If you pass the Certificate course, you will be eligible for the **Abridged Driving Theory Test**, which is a shorter driving theory test. Your eligibility will be valid for up to three years.

## Award

If you are studying for the Award, you will only study Units 1 and 2. They are exactly the same as Units 1 and 2 of the Certificate course.

## What will I need to know before taking the course?

This is a new course for all learners. No prior knowledge or experience is required.

## What kind of person should I be to take this course?

You should be a person who is keen to develop your own skills in being a safe road user. The course will require you to complete a number of short assignments and tests, so you should be hard working and motivated.

## What skills will I be using during the course?

You will be expected to plan and carry out tasks in which you will:

- identify, gather and record relevant information and evidence
- make judgements and present conclusions.

You will also need to use and further develop your personal learning and thinking skills. These are evidenced by being:

- an independent enquirer
- a creative thinker
- a team worker
- a reflector
- a self-manager
- an effective participant.

## How will the course help me?

This course will help you to be a safe road user. It may well also help you to safeguard your own life and the lives of others when you are travelling on the roads.

## Video and e-learning

As well as all the resources in this book, we have provided a companion website where you can view e-learning questions and video clips related to the units and created especially for this resource.

Access to the website is through the following URL:
www.contentextra.com/srsa

**Username:** srsa
**Password:** srsalevel1

# PREPARING FOR A SAFE JOURNEY BY ROAD

**Unit 1**

This unit promotes basic road safety and highlights the wide range of things you will need to consider when travelling on the roads. You will find out about the different forms of transport available and their costs and benefits. You will also learn how to recognise road types, read road maps, understand the costs of owning and maintaining a vehicle, and identify the different types of risk faced by road users. You will develop your knowledge and build your skills and, by the end of the unit, you will be able to successfully plan and prepare for a safe road journey.

After completing this unit you should:

- understand the costs and benefits associated with different forms of transport
- be able to plan a journey by road
- know the factors which affect risk and impair the performance of road users.

# CASE STUDY

# The D'Italia-Steven family goes to Cuba

The D'Italia-Steven family lives in Manchester and has just booked a two-week family holiday to Cuba. They fly from London Heathrow Airport in two weeks' time and are all very excited. Their flight leaves at 8.00 pm on a Friday evening.

The family is planning their journey to the airport and considering the different methods of transport they could use. Mum wants to travel by car but the journey will take at least four hours. Dad wants to take a train from Manchester to London and then use the London Underground to connect to the airport. One of the children has suggested travelling by bus, as there is a service which runs directly to the airport from Manchester.

The family cannot agree on the best way to travel.

## Thinking points

➔ Why is it important for the family to be sure of arriving at the airport on time?

➔ Plan a route for the family to use to get from Manchester to the airport if they decide to travel by car.

➔ Would you travel by car, train or bus? Explain your decision.

# The costs and benefits of travelling by different forms of transport

In this topic, you will learn about the different forms of transport available and their associated costs and benefits. People often consider only the financial costs of travelling and forget about the wider costs and benefits – for example, costs to health or to the environment. However, it is important to consider the bigger picture when deciding how to travel.

## Activity: Commuting to work

John commutes to and from work every day. He completes a 150-mile round trip in his car and he travels alone. John's travelling time each day is at least three hours.

1 Identify the different forms of transport commuters can use to travel to and from work.

2 Why might John prefer to travel to and from work alone, in his own car?

3 a Identify four advantages to John of using an alternative form of transport to travel to and from work.

  b Choose two modes of transport John could use and compare his journey to work. Think about cost, time and the environment.

### Think about it

- Which forms of transport have you used today?
- Were there alternative methods you could have used which might have been less stressful for you?
- Consider the possible effects of the transport you have used on:
  – the health and safety of others
  – the environment.

Is using the car always the best way to get to work?

## Common forms of transport used to make journeys in the UK

When deciding which form of transport to use, you will need to consider the distance to be travelled, the costs involved, and how quickly you need to reach your destination. The most common forms of transport in the UK are:

| car | motorbike/motor scooter | train |
|-----|-------------------------|-------|
| bus | bicycle | walking |

Two of the most popular forms of transport used for getting to college, work and enjoying our leisure time are the car and the train. In deciding which method of transport to use people often only consider short-term financial costs such as the petrol for the car or the price of the train ticket. There are many other cost implications to consider and it is important that we consider these when making decisions.

## The costs and benefits of different forms of transport

All forms of transport are associated with different costs and benefits. These can be split into five categories: financial, convenience, environmental, health and speed.

For example, a family of four, travelling from Leeds to London for a weekend break, might give the following reasons for travelling by train:

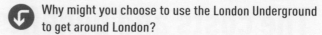 Why might you choose to use the London Underground to get around London?

| Financial | Convenience | Environmental | Health | Speed |
|---|---|---|---|---|
| Cheap family train ticket available | Train station close to where the family lives in Leeds | Space and social environment during the train journey | Travelling by train may be less stressful than driving | Journey will take only two hours |
| Cheap London Underground tickets for the weekend | Offer from a friend to take the family to the station | Less air pollution when travelling by train | More freedom to move about on the train | Smaller chance of delays than with motorway driving |
| Cost of car hire (the family does not currently own a car) | London Underground is convenient for getting to the hotel and travelling around London | Less use of non-renewable resources (e.g. oil) | | Time available for social activity in London on Friday night |
| Petrol/parking costs for car | | | | |

You may find it useful to complete this type of exercise when planning a journey. It will help you to see the true costs and benefits of one type of transport compared to others. Although door-to-door transport is attractive, you should consider the wider impact of your choices – for example, costs to your own health and the health of others.

# The efficiency and costs of different forms of energy sources

Different forms of transport are fuelled by a range of different energy resources. For example, cycling uses energy generated from the food you eat while a motorbike, car, train or bus may use electricity, petrol, diesel or liquid petroleum gas (LPG). Vehicles are often categorised according to the type of fuel they use and their engine size.

It is important to realise that all forms of transport use at least one form of energy. Car manufacturers are developing **hybrid cars** that use both petrol and electricity and these may seem more attractive than traditional cars. However, the electricity used by the hybrid car is often produced using **non-renewable resources** such as coal and oil, which are already in short supply. This is a hidden cost which the driver of a hybrid car may not consider.

# The social costs of road use

The different forms of transport you use also have a cost to the health of the nation. Every year, thousands of people are injured or die in road traffic accidents – for example, in the UK in 2010, there were around 36,000 emergency hospital admissions as a result of road traffic accidents. These incidents will have caused distress and anxiety for those involved, both at the time of the incident and (in many cases) in the longer term. It is impossible to estimate the true cost of these injuries to the people involved and to their families.

## Key terms

**Hybrid car** – a vehicle with both a traditional engine and a rechargeable system (battery) to improve mileage and reduce pollution.

**Non-renewable resources** – natural resources such as oil and coal, which when used are not replaced.

## Key safety information

- Always consider how the method of transport you use may affect your levels of stress and anxiety.

- Be aware of the wider costs of the transport method you choose, to other people in the community and to the wider environment.

## Just checking

1   Identify three forms of transport suitable for travelling to a local supermarket.

2   Identify two environmental or social costs of using a motorbike.

3   Outline the possible benefits of driving a hybrid car.

# The costs of private vehicle use

In this topic, you will learn about the costs associated with private vehicle use.

## Understanding vehicle costs

The costs associated with owning any type of vehicle can be split into three main categories: **initial costs**, **running costs** and end-of-life **disposal costs**.

## Initial costs

The cost of purchasing a vehicle is known as the initial cost or the starting-out cost.

The type of vehicle you are able to buy will depend largely on how much money you have to spend. Buying a small, second-hand car, for example, is a lot cheaper than buying a new, luxury, convertible sports car.

## Running costs

Most forms of transport will also cost money to run. Running costs may need to be paid daily, weekly, monthly or annually, and can be split into four main categories: taxation, servicing, insurance and fuel.

Running costs vary significantly between different forms of transport. For example, a basic road bike is relatively cheap to buy and to maintain. A moped, on the other hand, has a higher initial purchase cost but is still cheaper to run than the average family car.

> ### Key terms
>
> **Initial cost** – the cost of purchasing a form of transport.
>
> **Running cost** – the annual and everyday costs of a form of transport.
>
> **Disposal cost** – the cost of removing a form of transport from the road, track or airway, making sure that it doesn't pollute the environment and that as much as possible is recycled.

## Activity: Transport forms and costs

1 Identify which forms of transport shown above would involve an initial cost to an individual owner.

2 Which form of transport do you think is most expensive in terms of:

   **a** initial costs      **b** running costs      **c** disposal costs?

## Disposal costs

Disposal costs also vary significantly depending on the type of transport and the method of disposal. For example, you may be able to sell or trade in a vehicle you no longer need or want. You are unlikely to make a profit doing this, but you should be able to minimise your costs. If a vehicle is no longer serviceable or useable, however, you may need to pay a private company to collect and dispose of it. These companies will take the owner's logbook and issue the owner with a destruction certificate.

# Understanding the financial costs of private motor vehicles

Most young people look forward to owning a car but few fully understand the financial costs involved. The running costs of any vehicle are directly linked to the value of the vehicle, the size of the engine and the way in which the vehicle is driven and maintained. All of the costs below apply to cars, scooters and motorcycles.

- **Taxation:** Cars can be taxed for six or twelve months at a time, although it is cheaper to tax a car for a twelve-month period. The amount of tax paid is linked to the age of the car and the level of $CO_2$ emissions. Car tax is split by the government into 13 bands and some vehicles are exempt from car tax.
- **Servicing:** The servicing costs of a car will depend on the type of car, the number of miles travelled and the way in which the car is driven.
- **Insurance:** Insurance costs are linked to the size of the vehicle and the level of risk the driver presents to the insurance company. Insurance may be 'fully comprehensive' or 'third party, fire and theft'. The profile of the driver – for example, age, previous driving history, any medical conditions – will also affect the insurance cost.
- **Fuel:** Fuel costs will depend on the frequency of car use, the engine size and the way in which the car is driven.

All motor vehicles depreciate (lose value) as they get older.

 **Key safety information**

Ensure your vehicle is serviced at regular intervals, as directed in the vehicle handbook.

---

**Just checking**

1 Identify the three types of cost faced by transport owners.

2 Explain how car tax rates are set by the government. (You may need to do some additional research to answer this question fully.)

3 Describe three factors that will influence the cost of car insurance.

# Planning a safe road journey

In this topic, you will learn how to plan for a safe long-distance road journey. You will also consider the factors you need to take into account when planning a journey. It is possible to plan a successful journey and arrive at your destination without undue stress and anxiety.

## Different forms of transport

You can choose between a large number of transport methods – for example, walking, cycling, riding a horse, driving, or riding a motorbike or motor scooter. Each form of transport presents different risks, both to you as the transport user and to the road users around you.

> ### Key term
>
> **Comfort break** – a toilet/relaxation break.

## Initial travel planning

When preparing for a long journey, you will need to consider a number of factors which may make travelling easier. For example, you should think carefully about:

- which day of the week to travel on
- the time of day at which you travel.

If possible, avoid travelling during rush hour or on a Friday evening, since the roads are always busier at this time. You should also plan additional time in your travel schedule to allow for **comfort breaks**, poor weather, delays and other unforeseen circumstances. Never assume that your journey will be straightforward!

 Why is it so important to schedule comfort breaks into your journey plans?

 **Activity: Wedding travel**

Carlo and Chantelle, who live in Sunderland, have been invited to the wedding of their best friends in London. The wedding will take place at 2.00 pm on a Saturday and Carlo and Chantelle intend to travel there by car.

- Consider the factors they will need to take into account when planning and preparing for this journey.

## Preparing the route

It is very important to plan your route before you set out on any journey. Do you want to get to your destination as quickly as possible, or are you more interested in taking the scenic route? Some people plan detours so that they can stop at places of interest or make short visits to see friends.

There are a number of different planning options available. For example, you may plan your route using a satellite navigation system (satnav), an Internet route planner, a motoring organisation such as the Automobile Association (AA) or a map. It is a good idea to work out several possible routes to your destination, so that you have other options if driving conditions change due to poor weather, accidents, road closures or other incidents. Before setting out, you should also check for known delays caused by road works and/or accidents.

## The importance of planned breaks

On any long journey, it is vital to take regular breaks. Driving can be tiring and stressful, particularly in poor weather or late at night, and comfort breaks are essential. A quick break may prevent you from putting your own or others' safety at risk. Planned breaks will also give you a chance to update your travel information and prepare for changes in route due to unforeseen circumstances.

# Avoiding risk taking

If you fall behind schedule on a long journey, you may become stressed and anxious, particularly if the arrival time is important. Many drivers will try to make up for lost time and this may lead to risky manoeuvring, speeding, impatience behind the wheel and **tunnel vision**. If you are riding a motorcycle, you must avoid the temptation to weave in and out of traffic, since this will put you and other road users at risk. By building extra time into your travel schedule before you start, you can help to reduce stress and limit such dangerous behaviour.

**Key safety information**

- Plan your route for a journey well in advance of departure.
- When planning your journey schedule, remember to allow time for comfort breaks.
- Consider alternative routes to get to the same destination.

**Key term**

**Tunnel vision** – the loss of peripheral vision with the retention of central vision.

**Key safety information**

- People who speed or drive aggressively may not save time.
- Speeding involves accelerating hard but then braking hard.
- The journey may not be any quicker but fuel costs will definitely be higher.

**Just checking**

1  Identify three important factors to consider when planning a long journey.
2  Identify two sources of information which are available to help with route planning.
3  Describe two risky driving practices which may occur if a driver is trying to make up lost time during a journey.

# Using road maps to plan a journey

In this topic, you will learn about how to use road maps to plan a journey. Although satellite navigation systems (satnavs) are increasingly popular, you should be able to read a map.

## Road maps

There are many road maps available to buy and it is a good idea to keep a map with you when travelling, in case you need to use it. Most maps have an index which will help you to pinpoint where you are and where your destination is. Some maps also contain tables and charts to show the distances between major cities and towns and the estimated travel times from one to another.

Maps are drawn to scale so that they fit on the pages and use a **grid system** which will help you to find locations. The grid will also help you to see which direction you need to travel in. For example, if you are approaching a roundabout and you have the option of taking the M1 North or the M1 South, it is important to know the direction of your journey!

### Key term

**Grid system** – lines running horizontally and vertically on a map to help the user to pinpoint different locations.

## Activity: Planning a journey

Tariq and Ali are students studying at university in Sheffield. They are planning to visit some friends in Liverpool and intend to travel by motorbike.

1   Use a paper road map or an online journey planner to plan their route.
2   Build at least one comfort break into their journey.
3   Identify two stopping points where Tariq and Ali can visit places of interest.

## Road classifications and signs

During your journey, you may travel on several different types of road.

Motorways are major roads which connect different parts of the country. The M1, for example, connects the south of the country with the north. Motorways usually have three lanes for traffic travelling in each direction and are frequently used by travellers on long journeys as they allow for faster travel. Motorway signs have white writing on a blue background. Many motorways also

### Key safety information

- Always carry a map with you on long journeys.
- Use maps to plan in comfort breaks.

have electronic signs on gantries over the road. These signs show information such as changes to the speed limit, diversions or lane closures. You must watch these signs carefully in case something changes suddenly. Only certain types of vehicle are allowed on the motorways; for instance, cyclists and horse riders would be a real danger on a motorway so it is illegal to ride a horse or a bicycle on this type of road.

A roads are also major roads; many A roads were the main roads before motorways were built. These roads may have two or even three lanes for traffic travelling in each direction. Where these roads link major cities and towns, they are often referred to as **primary routes.** Signs on A roads have gold writing on a dark green background.

B roads are usually single lane and connect local areas (e.g. the B6148). Signs for B roads use black writing on a white background.

Temporary diversions are highlighted by yellow signs and tourist attractions by brown signs.

The type of road you travel on will often depend on how quickly you wish to get to your final destination and whether you need to stop off anywhere en route. The colour of the road signs you see will show what type of road you are travelling on. Driving tests in the UK now require candidates to follow road signs for themselves, without the support of the examiner, for part of the test.

> **Key term**
>
> **Primary route** – a major route between urban centres.

## Activity: How far?

Use a map or distance tables to calculate how many miles/kilometres it is between Glasgow and:

- London
- Manchester
- Southampton
- Leeds
- Bath.

---

**Just checking**

1  Identify three different types of road in the UK.

2  What colour sign is used to indicate a diversion from an established route?

3  Explain why it might be quicker to use B roads during rush hour, even though the total distance travelled may be greater.

# Everyday risks which impair the performance of road users

In this topic, you will learn about the everyday risks you face as a road user. These risks depend on the form of transport used, the type of road, your age and gender, and the time of day at which you choose to travel.

## Forms of transport

The method of transport you use to make a journey can present various risks to your own and others' safety. For example, in the event of an accident, the types of vehicle involved will have a significant impact on the outcome.

- A motorcyclist is more at risk than a car driver, because the motorbike provides less protection for the rider.
- The safety of a car driver may be affected by the length of the car's bonnet: the longer the bonnet, the more protection it offers in a head-on collision.
- Pedestrians, horses and horse riders and cyclists face the greatest risks if involved in an accident with a car.

As a general rule, the more physically exposed a road user is, the more personal risk they face. If a pedestrian is hit by a car travelling at 30 miles per hour, the pedestrian is likely to suffer serious or even fatal injury. By comparison, a bus passenger involved in an accident at a similar speed may experience much lower levels of injury.

## Road types

The risks you face are linked to the type of road you are travelling on (e.g. a motorway, a main road through a town). All road types present challenges and risks to road users but the causes of risk will be different in different environments.

The risks when driving in a town or city could be related to the increased number of vehicles on city roads and the increased number of distractions. On country roads, frustration caused by slow-moving vehicles such as tractors and bicycles can impair the performance of other road users, and risky decisions to overtake may place the driver involved – and other road users – at risk.

**Key safety information**

- Always drive within the given speed limit.

- Be patient with older drivers. They may be driving more slowly because they know that their reactions are not as good as when they were younger.

- If at all possible, avoid travelling during rush hour. It will reduce risks to your own safety.

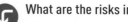 What are the risks in a situation such as this?

## Age and gender

Evidence has shown that younger road users are more at risk – and present a greater risk to other road users – because they have less experience. Road traffic accidents are one of the major causes of death for young males under the age of 25. Unfortunately, some people feel it is 'cool' to take risks on the road to impress their **peer group** and put their own and others' safety at a low priority. Older males are, statistically, much safer road users than younger males, although reaction times slow down in later adulthood (65+) and this affects safety on the roads.

> **Key term**
>
> **Peer group** – the social group you belong to.

 ## Activity: Car insurance

Daniel is 19 years old and has just passed his driving test. He has a clean licence and has never had an accident. His grandmother has bought him a brand new Mini car and he is looking for fully comprehensive insurance cover.

1  Use the Internet to find three different insurance quotes for Daniel.
2  What would the same insurance cost a 45-year-old man?
3  How would you account for the difference in cost? Do you think it is fair?

## Time of the day

As a road user, you can reduce risk by travelling at times when the roads are quieter. The highways tend to be busiest during peak periods in the morning and evening (i.e. rush hour). At weekends and in the middle of the day, the roads may be less congested, which should make driving less stressful.

## Speed

The legal maximum speed varies depending on the type of road you are using. It is important to realise that, when travelling at speed, you will have less time to make decisions and react to circumstances around you. For instance, it will take a lot longer to slow down if you are travelling at 70 miles per hour on a motorway than if you are travelling at 20 miles per hour on a B road. Excess speed can magnify the damage done when accidents occur so you should always stick to the speed limit.

 **Think about it**

1  Identify 'hotspots' – areas or situations where driving/walking/cycling/riding conditions are particularly stressful – you encounter during your journey to work or college.
2  What steps can you take to reduce the stress and anxiety these 'hotspots' may cause?
3  What effect might it have if you set off to drive home after a blazing row with someone you care about?

> **Just checking**
>
> 1  Identify two reasons why females may be safer road users than males.
> 2  Why might it be better to travel to work before rush hour in the morning?
> 3  Identify two ways in which horse riders can make themselves more visible to other road users.

# The physical states which impair the performance of road users

In this topic, you will learn how physical health, alcohol and **prescription** or **controlled drugs** affect and impair the performance of road users. There are strict laws about driving while under the influence of drugs or alcohol. For instance, if you cause the death of another person due to careless driving while under the influence of drugs or alcohol, you face a potential prison sentence of 14 years and a minimum obligatory two-year driving disqualification.

## Physical health

As a road user, you must be aware that your physical health has an effect on your ability to use the roads. Illness may affect your ability to concentrate fully and drive safely. Many people have ongoing health problems that they have to manage all the time, for example, diabetes or asthma. Do you know anybody who has an illness like this? If so, why not talk to them about how it might affect their ability to drive or ride safely.

Physical injuries may affect your mobility. For example, if you sprain your wrist during a football match, you may not be able to steer your car or bicycle safely. In this case, you will need to get a lift home and arrange to collect your own vehicle later.

## Alcohol

Alcohol will impair your performance and judgement on the road and if you drive or ride a vehicle while under the influence of alcohol, you will put yourself and others at risk. As a road user, you are very likely to encounter people who are drunk and you must be aware that they are likely to make unpredictable decisions, such as crossing the road without warning or changing lanes without indicating.

The UK legal limit for drivers is 80 mg of alcohol per 100 ml of blood. This is roughly equivalent to two pints of ordinary beer. However, even a small amount of alcohol in your bloodstream will affect your judgement as a road user. In Sweden, the upper allowed limit for drivers is 0.2 mg of alcohol per 100 ml of blood.

> **Key terms**
>
> **Prescription drug** – drug prescribed by a doctor for a specific purpose.
>
> **Controlled drug** – a drug prohibited by law and only allowed to be supplied under licence.

How can alcohol impair your driving or riding?

Alcohol affects your ability to react to situations and coordinate your actions. Alcohol makes it more difficult to judge speeds and distances accurately, which can increase the risk of accidents. If you have been drinking, you may also be overconfident and you are likely to overestimate your own ability to drive, cycle or walk. It may also make you more aggressive.

## Activity: Effects of alcohol

Alcohol may affect your:

| reaction times | judgement of distance |
|---|---|
| judgement of speed | confidence |
| coordination | decision making. |

1 Using the Internet, research one of the factors listed above and create a short PowerPoint® presentation to show how it will affect your ability to use the roads safely. Your presentation should be aimed at young people.

2 Discuss with some friends whether the UK should impose a total ban on drinking and driving.

**Key term**

**Reaction time** – the time between an event (e.g. a pedestrian stepping off the pavement into the road) and the driver's reaction.

The rate at which alcohol is broken down by the body is virtually the same for everybody, regardless of height, weight, gender or race. If you consume a large amount of alcohol, it will take over 10 hours for this to pass out of your system. This is why it is important not to drive the morning after an evening when you have had several drinks.

You should also be aware that it is illegal to ride a bicycle if you are over the drink drive limit. If you are caught cycling while drunk, you can be fined up to £2500.

## Prescription/controlled drugs

A survey carried out in 2006 found that young people are more likely to have been driven in a car by someone under the influence of drugs than by someone under the influence of alcohol. Controlled drugs are not freely available to the public but are sometimes taken illegally. Common examples include cannabis, ecstasy, cocaine and LSD. Some people feel that these drugs relax them, making them better drivers. The reality

**Key safety information**

- Never drive while under the influence of alcohol or drugs.

- Never get into a car being driven by someone whom you believe has been drinking or taking prescription drugs.

- Read the instructions of any medication/drugs prescribed to you to see whether they will have an impact on your performance as a road user.

is that they impair both the ability to make judgements and to control the vehicle. Even very small quantities of these drugs have an effect. If combined with alcohol, they can produce even more dangerous chemicals. Body-building drugs can also affect moods and concentration and may lead to aggressive behaviour towards other people.

 **How can prescription medication impair your performance as a road user?**

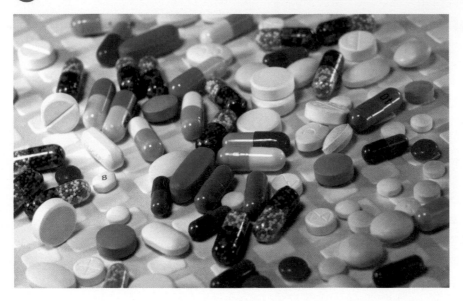

Prescription drugs are prescribed by a doctor to an individual for a specific purpose. If you are taking any prescription medication, you must read the accompanying leaflet to make sure it will not affect your ability to use the roads safely. Even common over-the-counter drugs for headaches and colds may cause drowsiness and slow down your reaction times. Some prescription drugs may react with alcohol so it is important to check before having an alcoholic drink.

People using drugs often struggle with multi-tasking activities. They will, therefore, find it difficult to ride a bicycle or horse, or to drive a motorbike or car. Hand–eye coordination is often affected and muscle control and concentration can also be impaired.

If you use the road while under the influence of drugs – legal or illegal – you will put yourself and the people around you at risk.

### Just checking

1  Is it ever safe to drink and drive/cycle/ride a horse etc?
2  Identify three effects of alcohol and drugs on the body.
3  Why is it safer to decide on a nominated driver at the beginning of a night out?

# The psychological states which impair the performance of road users

In this topic, you will learn how psychological states of mind can affect the performance of road users. **Fatigue** (or tiredness, as it is more commonly known) affects the ways in which you respond to the environment around you and slows your reactions to unexpected events. If you are upset or angry, this may affect your judgement and cause you to drive more aggressively than usual, which will have an impact on your own safety and the safety of the people around you.

**Key term**

**Fatigue** – tiredness.

## The effect of fatigue on the performance of road users

It is estimated about 20 per cent of all road accidents are linked to fatigue. Tiredness affects reaction times, concentration and your ability to focus, which can lead to accidents.

Common symptoms of fatigue include heavy eyelids, frequent yawning, erratic speed changes, drifting into other lanes and across lines on the road, misjudging situations, and general daydreaming.

## Activity: Too tired to drive?

Most people lead busy lives and experience various stresses and strains on a daily basis. There may be points during the week when your mental alertness is low, so it is important to be aware of these highs and lows.

1 Discuss with a friend the times during the week when you are likely to be tired.
2 Construct a table to identify the factors which cause this tiredness, and ways in which you might reduce these factors to ensure that you are more alert before using the roads.

The risk of fatigue is much higher at night because your body's natural rhythms make you want to sleep at this time. You are most likely to experience fatigue during long journeys. Fatigue is also common in the middle of the afternoon, particularly after a big lunch or if you have problems controlling your blood sugar levels, and early in the morning when people are groggy after waking up.

Driving has been shown to have a hypnotic effect on some people, causing them to lose concentration or fall asleep at the wheel. If you fall asleep for just a few seconds, you could travel hundreds of metres. Think what the consequences might be if you are on a bendy rural road or you are riding a motorcycle.

Many people find motorway driving tiring or hypnotic due to the volume of traffic on the road and the long, straight stretches. When driving on a motorway, you will need to make a lot of decisions – often quickly – as you respond to the actions of other road users. However, recent research has shown that driving on country roads can be equally tiring.

Older people tend to tire more quickly, so it is important for them to take more breaks during journeys to try to prevent the onset of fatigue.

### Key safety information

- If you are experiencing fatigue, you must take a break. It is a myth that opening the window or playing loud music will help.

- Be aware that newly qualified drivers lack experience on the road and this may account for what appears to be careful driving.

- Never distract the driver of a vehicle.

## Emotional states of mind and their effects on the performance of road users

As a road user, you must be aware that your emotional state can affect your judgement when you are using the road. For instance, it is unwise to set out on a journey if you are angry or upset about something. It is also important for drivers, riders and pedestrians to focus on the route they're taking, as a lapse in concentration could put other road users at risk. If you feel unable to concentrate, you should delay your journey until you are able to focus.

Distractions – whether inside or outside the vehicle – are one of the most common causes of accidents. For example, a group of friends travelling together in a car can easily distract the driver by messing around or drawing attention to something happening outside the car. If you are a passenger, it is important that you do not distract the driver; if you do, you will put yourself and other road users in danger. The risk of distraction is also why it is illegal to make calls or text on a mobile phone when driving.

 How can your passengers affect your safety on the roads?

## Activity: Graduated driving licence

**Graduated driving licences** are licences given to new drivers which include certain restrictions. The aim is to help new drivers to increase their skills and experience on the roads in a safe, controlled and low-risk environment.

The government and the Driving Standards Agency are particularly concerned about the safety of young drivers and are looking for ways to help them gain experience safely and quickly. Australia, New Zealand and parts of the USA have introduced Graduated Licence schemes as one response to this issue. A recent study by Cardiff University claims that restrictions on 17–24 year olds could prevent 1700 injuries a year and might help to lower car insurance premiums for drivers in this age group. However, it would be difficult and costly to police the scheme and it might make more people drive or ride without a licence or insurance. The right answer needs careful thought.

1 How effective do you think graduated driving licences would be in the UK?
2 What types of restriction would you impose on young drivers to improve road safety?

**Key term**

**Graduated driving licence** – a driving licence which includes restrictions for newly qualified drivers.

### Just checking

1 Identify three symptoms of fatigue that may be experienced by a road user.
2 Why can motorway driving be more stressful and tiring than travelling on A or B roads?
3 Identify three common situations in which a young road user is likely to be distracted by other people within the vehicle.

# The effects of the weather and travelling at night on road safety

In this topic, you will learn about how the weather and travelling at night can affect the safety of road users. **Visibility** is a key issue when travelling in the dark or in poor weather conditions such as rain or snow. Pedestrians, cyclists and motorcyclists may not realise how difficult it is for other road users to see them in low-light conditions.

## The effects of the weather in completing road journeys

Poor weather conditions can present a range of safety issues. Rain, fog, snow, ice or strong winds can turn a relatively stress-free journey into one which is both difficult and dangerous.

The table below highlights some of the issues that cyclists need to consider when completing a journey.

What difficulties have you encountered when travelling in bad weather?

| Road conditions | Possible dangers to the cyclist |
|---|---|
| Rain | Ability to see others, skidding/**aquaplaning**, visibility to other road users, stopping time/distances, the effects of cold and damp on the body, concentration levels, stress, difficulty in making judgements |
| Fog | Ability to see others, visibility to other road users, accidents, lack of concentration, stress, lack of awareness of what is happening on the roads generally |
| Snow | Ability to see others, skidding, stopping time/distances, visibility to other road users, the effects of the cold on the body, concentration levels, stress, difficulty in making judgements, cycling too fast |
| Ice | Accidents, skidding, dangers caused by **black ice**, stopping time/distances, cycling too fast |
| Strong winds | Stability of the bicycle, speed, headwinds/side winds and their possible effects, concentration levels, time needed to complete the journey |

Headwinds and side winds affect the stability of some vehicles and can result in road traffic accidents. Headwinds can reduce the speed of travel and side winds may cause vehicles to move unexpectedly across the highway and road lanes. This presents a particular danger to those road users who are exposed to the elements, such as motorcyclists and cyclists. In poor driving conditions where there are strong winds, bridges are sometimes closed to high-sided vehicles and extra speed limits may be imposed.

## Activity: Poor weather conditions

Poor weather conditions affect the safety of all road users.

- Consider two forms of transport which you use regularly and assess the possible dangers you might face in poor weather conditions. You may wish to construct two tables similar to the one on the previous page.

## Completing a journey in the dark

Travelling at night presents various challenges for road users when it comes to ensuring their own safety and the safety of others. Roads in city centres are usually well lit, but in some rural areas there is no street lighting and country roads are often left in the dark. In some parts of the UK, stretches of motorway are also left unlit.

If you are walking, jogging or cycling at night, you should wear a luminous yellow **tabard** to increase your visibility to other road users. Cyclists should use the correct lights on their bicycles. Drivers should also have a luminous tabard in their car at all times, so that they will be visible if they have to wait at the side of the road following a breakdown.

### Key safety information

- Walkers, joggers and cyclists must wear a luminous tabard if using the roads at night.

- Scooter, moped and motorbike riders should wear high-visibility clothing.

- Adjust your driving actions as necessary in poor weather conditions or in the dark. In bad weather, you should turn your lights on.

- Be aware of the ways in which weather conditions may affect the actions of other vehicles on the road.

### Key term

**Tabard** – a short, usually sleeveless, jacket often placed over an outer coat.

### Just checking

1 Identify two ways in which a horse rider can increase their visibility to other road users.
2 Consider the actions a motorcyclist will need to take in times of high wind.
3 Discuss with a friend the factors which need to be taken into consideration when driving in snowy or icy conditions.

# Assessment overview

While working through this unit, you will have prepared for the following assessment tasks:

| 1.1 | Comparing the costs and benefits of two forms of transport | Pages 3–7 |
|-----|-----|-----|
| 2.1 | Planning a long distance road journey using appropriate information sources and technology | Pages 8–9 |
| 2.2 | Planning a long distance journey using map reading skills | Pages 10–11 |
| 3.1 | Describe the different factors which affect the risk of accidents on a planned journey | Pages 12–13 |
| 3.2 | Identify the physical and psychological states of mind which can affect our ability to use the roads | Pages 14–19 |
| 3.3 | Identify how weather conditions and travelling at night may affect safety | Pages 20–21 |

edexcel
advancing learning, changing lives

# Assignment tips

➜ **Task 1.** To meet the assessment criteria, you will need to select two forms of transport and compare them using the same journey (from a to b), at least in terms of finance, environment and speed. You may wish to look at other factors as well, but you must cover these three factors as a minimum.

➜ **Task 2.** To meet the assessment criteria, you will need to plan journeys to two different destinations. These destinations must be unfamiliar and your journeys must involve the use of private transport. You will need to use a range of road types and build in scheduled stops. The first journey will need to use technological tools but the second journey must rely on printed maps.

➜ **Task 3.** To meet the assessment criteria, you will need to demonstrate your knowledge of the factors which affect risk and impair the performance of road users. You may wish to demonstrate your knowledge and understanding of these factors by linking this section to one of your planned journeys. You might highlight the risks in one of your planned journeys and suggest ways in which these risks could be reduced. You will also need to produce materials, such as a PowerPoint® presentation, to show how specific factors place the road traveller at risk. You will need to cover at least three of the following features: alcohol, temporary physical impairment, fatigue, emotional states, weather, night-time road use and distraction.

# Maintaining own and others' safety in relation to vehicles

This unit promotes safety for users and passengers of all forms of road transport. You will learn about vehicle checks and maintenance and about how to respond in the case of breakdowns or accidents.

After completing this unit you should:

- know the regular checks that need to be carried out on a form of transport
- be able to carry out safety checks on a form of transport
- know how to respond in cases of breakdowns and accidents.

# Ruben checks the car before travelling to Plymouth

Ruben and his partner live in Aberdeen, in Scotland. They have two young children and a pet dog called Molly. Ruben is taking the whole family to visit his sister in Plymouth, in the south of England. To make the trip, he has borrowed a car from a close friend and purchased fully comprehensive car insurance for a week.

Before the family departs, Ruben carries out some routine checks on the car, to prepare for the journey. It is winter, and the family is travelling in the evening, so Ruben cleans the car lights at the front of the vehicle, checks he has enough windscreen washer fluid and fills the car up with petrol. He decides not to check the oil and brake fluid levels because his friend says he checked them last week.

## Thinking points

➡ Why is it important to complete routine checks on any vehicle before setting out on a long journey?

➡ Ruben cleaned the front lights, looked at the level of windscreen washer fluid and filled the car up with petrol. Why do you think he focused on these checks?

➡ Do you think Ruben has carried out the right checks before such a long journey?

➡ Are there any other checks you would have considered completing before you started out on this journey?

➡ The family is taking Molly, their dog, with them. Do they need to consider any other safety checks for the vehicle?

# Regular checks that need to be carried out on a car

In this topic, you will learn about the regular checks and maintenance that need to be carried out on a car. You will also learn why these checks need to be carried out. It is the responsibility of all car users to make sure that their vehicle is roadworthy and working effectively. If these checks are not done regularly the safety of the driver, passengers, pedestrians and other vehicle users is put at risk.

## Common checks and maintenance for cars

The number of cars on UK roads has increased greatly over the years. It is estimated that there are over 31 million cars on the roads today. With so many cars on the road, it is important for all car owners to keep their vehicles roadworthy. Information about which checks need to be carried out – and how often – is provided in the car owner's handbook. You should read this handbook carefully and get to know the checks that need to be completed. All makes and types of car are different, but there are common checks that all drivers need to ensure are completed.

### Tyres

It is estimated that more than three-quarters of all cars on the road in the UK at any one time have incorrect tyre pressures. In 2010, over a thousand road accidents were directly related to defective tyres. Tyre pressure and the condition of the tyres affect the stopping distance of the car, the car's grip on the road and the possibility of having a **blowout**.

Car tyres must be in good condition and fit for road use. The tread depth must be above the legal limit of 1.6 mm, in a continuous band in the centre three-quarters of the tread and around the whole circumference of the wheel. Car tyres must also be inflated to the correct level. Poor tyre pressure will mean that the driver uses more fuel; it is estimated that over 370 million litres of fuel are wasted each year in the UK, due to incorrect tyre pressures. This increase in fuel consumption also creates an additional 1 million tonnes of **$CO_2$ emissions** each year, which contributes to air pollution.

Your car handbook will help you to identify the correct pressures for the front and back tyres; these pressures may be different and they may change if you are carrying a heavy load. You should check the tyre pressure when the tyres are cold, taking into account the weight being carried in the vehicle.

> **Key terms**
>
> **Blowout** – a sudden bursting of the tyre.
>
> **$CO_2$ emissions** – carbon dioxide pollution.

## Activity: Too much pressure?

Car tyres may be over-inflated, under-inflated or correctly inflated. Tyre pressure affects the handling of the car.

1 Choose four different cars of different types and with different engine sizes.
2 Identify the correct tyre pressures for each of these vehicles.
3 Research the possible consequences of over-inflation and under-inflation of car tyres.
4 Research the ways in which poor steering and suspension may affect tyre wear patterns.

## Lights

Car lights need to be in good condition so that the driver can see clearly when driving at night or in poor weather conditions. You must keep your car's lights clean and make sure that all front and back lights are working effectively. Most modern vehicles have some kind of indication on the dashboard which will tell you if there is a lighting fault; make sure you replace any broken bulbs as soon as possible – you may be committing an offence if you do not.

Good lighting will enable you to see and be seen by other vehicles and road users. However, you must show consideration to other people when driving at night and make sure your lights are adjusted so that they do not dazzle other road users. Some vehicles are fitted with lights that stay on during daylight hours or come on automatically. You should not tamper with these lights or try to override them. This may damage the electrical system of the car.

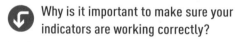

Why is it important to make sure your indicators are working correctly?

## Indicators

Indicator lights allow you to warn other road users that you are about to change direction or slow down. It is important to check (daily, if possible) that your indicators are working properly and that the lens is showing the correct colour; otherwise, there is an increased risk of road traffic accidents. In some cars, it is possible to replace indicator bulbs easily; however, you may need to visit an appropriate car dealer so that they can fit the new bulb (or bulbs) for you.

## Oil level

You should check the oil level in your car twice a month: without the correct level of oil, the engine will not run properly and can be severely damaged. When checking the oil level in a car, the vehicle must be parked on a flat surface and the engine should be cold. Insert the dip stick (usually found under the car bonnet) into the oil reservoir and check that the oil level is between the minimum and maximum indicators on the dip stick. Top up the oil if necessary, but be careful not to overfill – too much oil is as bad as too little. Some cars monitor the oil level via the onboard computer. You must read your vehicle handbook to find out which icon on the instrument panel will light up if the oil level drops.

## Brake fluid

It is important to check the brake fluid level on a regular basis. Being able to brake effectively is one of the most important aspects of driving. The brake fluid cylinder should be filled to the 'full' line with the correct type of brake fluid. You can find out what type of brake fluid you need in the vehicle handbook. If you are not confident about what to do, leave it to somebody who is, such as a garage mechanic. The cleanliness of the brake fluid should also be checked when the vehicle is serviced.

## Water coolant and washer fluid

The water coolant in a car's radiator is the most important part of the car's system for cooling the engine down. The coolant level should always be kept at the manufacturer's recommended level. Maximum and minimum levels are indicated on the coolant reservoir. If the engine overheats, this may cause a breakdown which may lead to very expensive repairs. Check the coolant reservoir weekly and remember that the recommended ratio of water to **antifreeze** varies depending on the weather conditions and the type of antifreeze you are using. In winter, the ratio should be 50:50 water to antifreeze, to make sure the engine is protected in the cold weather.

The windscreen washer cylinder must also be topped up regularly, as vision is crucial. It is important to add antifreeze – especially in winter – so that the liquid flows freely and does not freeze as it reaches the windscreen. Buy antifreeze designed for this purpose. It may not be appropriate to use the same antifreeze in your washers as you do in your cooling system. On long journeys, it is possible to use a whole cylinder of windscreen fluid – especially if the weather is bad and there is a lot of salt on the roads and spray from other vehicles – so you should top up the washer fluid before setting out.

> ### Key term
>
> **Antifreeze** – a liquid added to the water coolant system of a vehicle, and to windscreen fluid, to prevent it from freezing in winter.

## Windscreens and windscreen wipers

Cracks and chips in the windscreen can badly affect the driver's vision and should be repaired as quickly as possible to ensure road safety. Regular checks of the screen are important; in some instances, specialists will be able to repair chips easily without having to replace the whole windscreen.

Fully functioning windscreen wipers are also essential and a car will fail its MOT if the windscreen wipers are faulty. This is because the driver presents a risk to themselves and to other road users if they cannot see properly. Generally, windscreen wipers should be replaced if they leave bands of rain on the windscreen, make a noise or judder. Blades should be cleaned weekly with detergent, and dirt and grit should be removed.

### Key safety information

- Always check tyre pressures, oil levels and liquid fuel levels regularly.

- Ensure windscreen wipers work effectively.

- Replace car light bulbs as soon as possible after you find out that they are no longer working.

### Just checking

1  Is the tyre tread depth on your car currently legal?

2  Do you know what the tyre pressure should be for your car for everyday journeys?

3  Have you checked your tyre pressures in the last two months?

4  What are the possible consequences of not completing these simple checks regularly? If you do not have your own car, carry out these checks on a friend's or parents' car.

# Regular checks that need to be carried out on a motorcycle, moped or scooter

 What regular checks need to be carried out on a motorcycle?

In this topic, you will learn about the regular checks and maintenance that need to be carried out on motorcycles, mopeds and scooters. You will also learn why these checks need to be carried out. These vehicles require specific checks that are different from those of car users, and these are important for ensuring the safety of motorbike and moped riders and of other road users. Motorcyclists and moped riders are up to 30 times more likely to die on the roads than drivers of any other vehicle.

## Common checks and maintenance for motorbikes and mopeds

### Tyres
Tyre pressures should be checked regularly using a gauge. The tread depth of motorcycle tyres must be 1 mm deep for a band at least three-quarters of the width of the tyre. If you ride a motorcycle, you must check – daily, if possible – for bulges, tears or foreign objects (such as nails ) in the tyres.

### Brake fluid and the brakes
You must check the brake fluid reservoir regularly to make sure the fluid level is between the high and low markings. The condition of the brake fluid should also be checked, since dirt and water in the brake fluid can affect the performance of the vehicle.

If you are a motorcyclist, you should also look out for excessive brake lever and brake pedal travel, and pay attention to signs of unusual play or sponginess. These are good indicators that something is wrong with the brakes and should be dealt with quickly. An effective braking system is essential and regular checking could save your own life and the lives of other road users.

### Chain
You must check that the chain or belt of your motorcycle has the correct tension and is aligned to the rear wheel correctly. Information about tension can be found in the motorcycle handbook. **Lubricant** is needed to prevent excessive wear of the chain. If lubricant is not used, the links in the chain are likely to seize up; this may cause the chain to break, which could lead to a serious accident.

---

**Key term**

**Lubricant** – a substance that reduces friction and makes things slippery.

---

## Lights and indicators

Most accidents involving motorcyclists occur because the other road user(s) involved did not see the motorcycle. Therefore, if you ride a motorcycle or moped, you must make sure that **daylight running lights**, night lights, brake lights and reflectors are clean, functional and emitting the correct colour. These will increase your **visibility** to other road users and allow you to show your intentions if you are about to slow down or change direction.

You should also make sure that all four hazard lights are working, in case you break down. About 10 per cent of motorcycle MOT failures are due to ineffective lights, but these are some of the easiest checks to make on a motorcycle. These checks should be carried out daily if possible.

## Suspension

It is important to check the suspension on your motorcycle or moped as this ensures that the motorcycle runs smoothly. If the suspension is incorrect, the motorbike will not handle as well as it might and tyre wear will increase. The suspension should be checked on a weekly basis and adapted as necessary to suit the road surface and the conditions. Do not adjust the suspension unless you are confident about what to do. If in doubt, take your vehicle to a professional.

 What should you do if you think there is a problem with your vehicle?

> **Key terms**
>
> **Daylight running lights** – lights that stay on all day to increase visibility without dazzle.
>
> **Visibility** – the quality of being able to be seen by the eye.

## Exhaust

A faulty exhaust will increase noise and $CO_2$ pollution to the environment, so you should check for holes or other faults regularly. You should also make sure the exhaust is secure and not affecting the rear suspension. In the MOT test for a motorcycle, the exhaust will be checked to make sure its noise level is legal.

## Suitability of helmet and clothing

Riders of motorcycles and mopeds are very exposed, so it is important that they wear the correct clothing. A legally compliant helmet is required by law and must be worn to protect against head injury if the driver falls off the motorcycle or is involved in an accident. You should check the safety rating of your helmet by looking at the Safety Helmet Assessment and Rating Programme (SHARP). Replace your helmet if it is damaged.

You should also wear boots to help prevent foot and ankle injuries; these boots should ideally be made of a tough material with rigid soles, so you can get a good grip. Motorcycle jackets and trousers should be made of leather, Kevlar® or nylon, with heavy padding and additional spine protectors. You should also wear gloves to protect your hands from damage or the cold. Ideally, the clothes you wear should also improve your visibility to other road users.

**Key safety information**

- Always wear suitable clothing and a helmet. Your life may depend on it.

- Ensure your indicators are working so that other road users are aware of your intentions.

- Check your brake fluid level on a regular basis.

- Ensure that any passengers you carry also wear appropriate clothing and a helmet for safety.

## Activity: Heads first!

You have just bought your first moped and are keen to get on the road.

1  Research the different types of motorcycle helmet available to buy.

2  Select an appropriate helmet from those available. Prepare a brief presentation, to be given to a friend, explaining why you have selected this particular helmet.

**Just checking**

1  What are the possible consequences of faulty motorcycle lighting for other road users?

2  Why is it important that all motorcycle passengers wear the correct clothing at all times?

3  Why is it important to get your vehicle checked if you think there is something wrong with the suspension?

# Regular checks that need to be carried out on a bicycle

In this topic, you will learn about the regular checks and maintenance that need to be carried out on a bicycle. You will also learn why these checks need to take place. Bicycles are one of the most common forms of transport used by young people and cyclists are some of the most vulnerable people on the road.

## Common checks and maintenance for bicycles

### Tyres

Your bicycle tyres should be correctly inflated so that the bike rides smoothly. You should barely be able to squeeze the side wall of the tyre with your finger and thumb: if you are able to do this, your tyres are too soft. The tyres must have 3 mm tread and no cracks or splits. If the tyres are cracked or split, punctures are more likely. It is also useful to check that the tyres are not rubbing against the frame of the bicycle; this could stop the wheel turning properly or damage the tyre, leading to a puncture. A sensible cyclist will make these checks daily – they only take a few minutes, but they can make a big difference.

### Brakes

You must check that your bicycle's brakes are working correctly; otherwise, you will endanger yourself and other road users. You should check the brake cables to make sure they are not frayed and there is not too much 'give'. You should be able to apply both brakes without too much effort and the brake levers must be attached firmly to the handlebars. The brake blocks must not be over worn and they must not touch the wheel rims when the brakes are off.

### Chain

You should check your bicycle chain regularly as this turns the wheels and allows you to change gear. The chain must be lubricated so that the links do not seize up – this could cause the chain to break. You should also make sure the chain cannot come off the front or back wheels and that the tension is no more than 25 mm.

 What regular checks need to be carried out on a bicycle?

 **Key safety information**

- Complete a general all-round check on your bicycle at least once a week.

- Ensure the chain is well lubricated and the brakes work effectively.

- Clean your lights and reflectors daily.

- Always wear clothing that ensures you are visible to other road users.

## Lights and reflectors

If you are riding your bicycle on the roads, you must have lights. At dusk and when it is dark, it will be almost impossible for other road users to see you if you do not have lights. These lights should be firmly attached to the frame, and you should check them regularly to make sure they cannot fall off or swing into the wheel. At night, your bicycle must have a white front light, a red rear light and a red rear **reflector**. All lights and reflectors should be kept clean and checked daily to ensure they are fit for purpose.

## Helmet and clothing

Cyclists can be very difficult to see, especially when it is dark or if the weather is bad. When you are cycling, you should always wear clothing that will make you more visible to other road users – for example, a brightly coloured, luminous jacket, preferably with reflective strips.

## Activity: Dressing safely

Research and suggest appropriate clothing for a 15-year-old cyclist.

Consider the folllowing factors:

- visibility
- protection from the weather
- protection in case of an accident.

Cyclists should wear a **cycling helmet** to protect their skull in case of an accident. Your helmet must fit properly, be light and not affect your vision. A well-fitting helmet will sit securely on your head; the strap should fit under your jaw with no more than one finger width between the strap and your throat. If your helmet is damaged, you should replace it as soon as possible.

### Key terms

**Bicycle reflector** – a small object which reflects light from other vehicles and draws attention to the cyclist, making them more visible to other road users.

**Cycling helmet** – a helmet specially designed to protect the head of a cyclist.

### Just checking

1 Identify two common faults with a bicycle which could affect its road worthiness.
2 How can cyclists make themselves more visible to other road users?
3 Why do you think child and young adult cyclists are at the highest risk of road traffic accidents?

# Regular checks that need to be carried out on a horse

In this topic, you will learn about the regular checks that need to be made to ensure your safety if you intend to ride a horse on the roads. Remember also that a horse may seem calm but could react suddenly and in unexpected ways if startled. You will need to learn what you can do to reduce the risk of this happening. The British Horse Society runs training courses designed to prepare you and your horse for road riding.

No one knows the exact number of riders using the roads. What we do know is that other road users are often unsure about how to handle the situation when they encounter one or a number of horses.

## Suitability of clothing

If you ride a horse on the road, you must make sure you are visible to other road users. Light-coloured or fluorescent clothing is needed during the daytime and reflective clothing is needed if you intend to ride at night or in poor weather conditions. (It is safer not to ride at night or in poor weather conditions but on some occasions this may be necessary.) When riding, you should wear a band – white to the front and red to the rear – around your right arm or leg/riding boot. You could attach small LED lights to the back of your jacket or helmet. This will help other road users to see you.

You should ensure that your horse is fully visible as well, by fitting reflective bands just above the horse's fetlocks, as in the image. It is also recommended that your horse wears a fluorescent tabard and a fluorescent or reflective tail guard.

If you are leading your horse on the roads at night, it is recommended that you carry a light in your right hand which is white to the front and red to the rear.

## Suitability of helmet

All horse riders should wear a helmet to protect their skull in case of an accident; children under the age of 14 must wear a securely fastened helmet by law. It is best to buy a helmet that complies with The British Horse Society standards and have it professionally fitted.

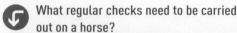
What regular checks need to be carried out on a horse?

### Activity: Buying a helmet

Nasreen and Amir have two children aged thirteen and seven. Both children have decided to take up riding and have been advised to buy their own helmets.

1 Research the types of helmet available for the children to buy.

2 Select the two helmets you think are most suitable for the children. Explain the benefits of each helmet so that Nasreen and Amir can make an informed choice about which one to buy.

### Key safety information

- Always wear fluorescent and reflective clothing when riding on the roads.

- Avoid riding on the roads at night if possible.

- A body protector would protect your spine and ribcage if you fell.

### Key terms

**Tack** – the accessories worn by horses, for handling and safety purposes.

**Bridle** – a harness fitted round the horse's head, used to guide the horse and restrain it if necessary.

**Traction** – the grip between the horse's hooves and the road surface.

## Tack

Before taking your horse on the road, you must make sure the **tack** fits well and is in good condition. These checks need to be done to ensure that you are in control of the horse and do not place other road users in danger. Never ride a horse without a saddle and **bridle**, and check all the tack regularly (ideally at least once a week).

 What can you do to improve your horse's grip on the roads?

## Hooves

If your horse does not have metal shoes fitted, make sure its hooves are in good condition. This will reduce the possibility of the horse stumbling on the road. Metal horse shoes may make it more difficult for the horse to 'grip' the smooth road surface so, if you regularly ride your horse along roads, it is a good idea to fit 'road studs' in the metal shoes to increase **traction**.

### Just checking

1 Why is it unwise to ride a horse on the roads at night or in poor weather conditions?

2 As a rider, how should you prepare your horse before riding on the road?

3 What actions should horse riders take to ensure their visibility to other road users?

# Carrying out regular checks on vehicles safely

In this topic, you will learn about the different factors you need to take into account when carrying out safety and maintenance checks on a form of transport. It is the owner's responsibility to ensure checks are carried out and to ensure that they do not put themselves, their passengers or other road users at risk. When completing vehicle checks, you must follow appropriate procedures.

## Activity: Check those levels!

Elise is helping her friend Luc to complete some basic checks on his car before he sets off on a long journey.

1  Before they do anything, what sort of reading should Elise and Luc do?
2  Which manual will they need with them to complete their checks effectively?
3  How should Elise and Luc dress when carrying out these checks?
4  What sort of 'physical resources' will Elise and Luc need in order to maintain the vehicle and prepare it for the long journey?

## Learning how to complete safety checks

There are basic rules and procedures that need to be followed when completing safety checks. When you first purchase any form of transport, it is important to learn how to complete these checks.

## Following basic safety rules

Before completing any checks or maintenance, ensure the vehicle is off the road and in a secure place. If the vehicle has an engine, this needs to be switched off and the keys removed from the ignition. This ensures that you are safe and that others cannot start the vehicle while you are completing your checks. If the vehicle has just been used, you will need to allow the engine to cool down so that it is safe for you complete the checks.

When you are checking fluid levels, the vehicle will need to be on a flat surface to ensure an accurate reading. Oil checks need to be completed shortly after the vehicle has been used and the oil has been pumped round the engine system. This gives a more accurate reading. It is always useful to have a second person available to help with basic checks on motor vehicles such as checking that indicators and other lights work.

## Using handbooks and Internet guides

Before you complete any basic maintenance or safety checks, it is a good idea to read the vehicle **handbook** or any other written resources about the vehicle. These resources will outline clearly the checks that need to take place, how often they need to be carried out and how to complete them. Always keep handbooks and guides close at hand so that you can refer to them when you need to.

There is a range of resources and checklists available on the Internet, explaining how to complete basic maintenance. They often give step-by-step instructions which can be very useful.

## Observation of others completing checks and maintenance

Many people learn best by watching others carry out maintenance and safety checks before they do them alone. Ask for help from a qualified professional, such as a car mechanic, if you are in doubt about how to complete a check. Most garages will take the buyer of a vehicle through the range of regular checks they need to carry out before they leave with the vehicle; many will also offer support after the purchase as well.

Road users often ask for support from other adults and friends who may be able to offer help and advice. Parents, for example, often work with their children and teach them how to complete basic bicycle checks and repairs. However, you should never rely on what other people say: it is your responsibility to ensure your vehicle is well maintained and safe for the road.

## Listening to professionals

Many local colleges offer short courses on vehicle maintenance. You may find it helpful to go on one of these courses, to increase your knowledge and understanding of basic safety checks and maintenance.

**Key term**

**Handbook** – a concise book of instructions about a vehicle which is used by the owner.

**Key safety information**

- Always ensure that any form of transport is off the road before safety checks are completed.

- Ensure that the engine is turned off and the keys removed from the ignition when checking motor vehicles.

- If in any doubt, ask a professional.

How can you learn how to carry out maintenance and safety checks on your vehicle?

**Just checking**

1   Where would be a suitable place to complete safety checks on a vehicle before using the roads?
2   Identify two occasions when you might need to take your vehicle to a garage rather than carrying out basic maintenance checks alone.
3   Which safety checks require more than one person?

# Responding safely at breakdowns

In this topic, you will learn how to respond if your vehicle breaks down on the road or motorway. It is estimated that on a typical day in the UK, one car breaks down every nine seconds; this number will be even higher in difficult weather conditions during the winter period. Breakdowns can put the driver, passengers and other road users in danger, so you should know how to respond and what action to take.

## Activity: Seeking help

Aoife is walking her dog along a main road when she is approached by a woman with two young children. The woman speaks very little English but is able to explain that her car has broken down. She is unsure what to do.

1 What advice should Aoife give to the woman?
2 How can she help to ensure the family's safety?

## Selecting a safe place to stop

If you break down, it is important to consider the safety of yourself and other road users. Motorcycles and bicycles should be removed from the highway as quickly and as safely as possible. Dealing with a car breakdown may be much more difficult. If possible, get your car off the road and warn others about what you are doing by using your **hazard warning lights**.

If you are driving on a motorway and develop a problem, leave at the first possible exit or pull in to a service area. If you cannot do this, pull on to the hard shoulder and position the vehicle as far to the left as possible. Try to stop near an emergency telephone. If you cannot get your vehicle onto the hard shoulder, switch on your hazard warning lights and only leave your vehicle when you have a clear view of the motorway and see that it is safe to do so.

### Key term

**Hazard warning lights** – lights on a vehicle that blink on and off to draw the attention of other road users in cases of breakdowns and accidents.

### Did you know?

In some European countries it is illegal not to carry a fluorescent tabard with you in a car.

# Remaining safe

It is useful to have a fluorescent, reflective tabard in your car at all times, which you can wear if you break down. This will make you more visible to other road users. Make sure you leave your vehicle from the left-hand side and ensure that your passengers do the same. This will reduce the risk to yourself and to other road users. Always stand in a safe place while you wait for assistance.

If you break down on the motorway, drive your vehicle on to the hard shoulder and stand well clear of the vehicle and the motorway lanes. Make sure that all your passengers do the same and that children are well supervised.

If you have an animal with you, it should be left in the vehicle unless the situation is dangerous. If you have to remove the animal from the vehicle, you must make sure it is kept under proper control.

# How to warn other road users of a breakdown

If your car breaks down on a road other than a motorway, place a warning triangle 45 metres behind the vehicle, on the same side of the road. Other road users will then be aware of the situation. You need to do this with care for your own and others' safety. If possible, keep the vehicle sidelights on at night or if the weather conditions are poor. Make sure that neither you, nor your passengers, stand between the vehicle and oncoming traffic. If the weather conditions are poor, do not stand in a position where you are obstructing your warning lights.

# Seeking assistance

If you have a mobile phone, you should make sure this is fully charged before any long journey. If you break down, you will need to phone someone else for support (once you have made yourself, your passengers and your vehicle as safe as possible). It is a good idea to take out breakdown cover (for example, by joining the AA or the RAC) so that you are guaranteed support if you break down.

If you are on a motorway and don't have a mobile phone, you will need to walk to the emergency telephone on your side of the carriageway and seek support. This telephone is free to use and puts you in contact with either the **Highways Agency** or the police. They will ask for your location and come to offer

---

**Key term**

**Highways Agency** – part of the Department for Transport which supports drivers who break down on the roads and motorways in England.

Do you know how to use the emergency telephones on the motorway?

you support. You should return to your vehicle until support arrives, although you may also wish to telephone your own breakdown service at this time.

If you feel your personal safety is at risk from another road user, return to your vehicle from the left-hand side and lock all the doors until the danger has passed.

## Disabled drivers

If you have a disability which prevents you from getting out of your vehicle safely and your vehicle breaks down you should stay in your vehicle. Switch on your hazard warning lights and if possible display the pennant 'Help' sign. If you have a car phone or mobile phone, contact the emergency services and ask for the police or the Highways Agency.

### Key safety information

- Always move a broken-down vehicle off the highway if it is safe to do so.

- Warn other road users about the breakdown by using warning lights and a warning triangle.

- The safest way to call for help is to get out of your vehicle, move well away from the carriageway and use your mobile phone or an emergency telephone.

- If you feel personally unsafe in a breakdown situation, return to your car and lock all the vehicle doors. Let the breakdown company know so they can treat your case as a priority.

### Just checking

1  How can the driver of a car make themselves and their vehicle visible to other road users?
2  Why is it important to fully charge your mobile telephone before setting out on a long journey?
3  Why is it advisable to purchase breakdown cover if you own a motor vehicle?

# What to do at the scene of an accident

In this topic, you will learn about how to respond at the scene of a road traffic accident. As a road user, you must know what to do if you are involved in or a witness to an accident.

## When and where to stop

At a road traffic accident, the owners of all vehicles involved should stop and remain near their own vehicle. This is so that personal details can be exchanged between the people involved.

Road users also need to stop if:

- a person other than themselves is injured
- another person's property or vehicle is damaged
- an animal running across the road or in another vehicle is injured
- a street lamp, bollard or other part of public property is damaged.

Perhaps the most important thing to do at the scene of an accident is to remain calm and to make sure that the people involved are as safe as possible. If the accident is on a busy road or a motorway, you should also try to make the accident scene safe for other road users. Ensure that the vehicle or vehicles involved are visible, using hazard warning lights and warning triangles, and wear reflective clothing yourself. Switch off all engines and make sure nobody smokes.

It is important that the people involved in the accident move to a safe place close to the road and that other road users are warned of the situation. If possible, a warning triangle should be placed 45 metres behind the vehicle. Do not attempt to move any casualties from their vehicle unless further danger is threatened. Do not try to remove a motorcyclist's helmet. You should only move a vehicle that has been involved in an accident if it is absolutely necessary and safe to do so. If you have had a gentle shunt and the vehicles are still drivable, it may be possible to move to a safer place. If, the accident is more serious and people are injured or trapped, you should leave things where they are until the emergency services arrive. If nobody is injured or trapped and you believe there is a need to move a vehicle to prevent another accident, ensure that the engine is off and there is no **fuel leakage**. A spark in this situation could start a fire. If possible, it is always better to let the emergency services make the decision about moving a vehicle.

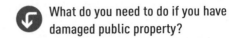

What do you need to do if you have damaged public property?

**Key term**

**Fuel leakage** – the spillage of petrol or diesel on the highways

41

# What information will be useful to the emergency services

Some serious accidents will require the support of some or all the emergency services (e.g. police, ambulance and fire services). These services work together as a team. To contact them, you will need to ring 999 or 112. Do not use a mobile phone if there is petrol spillage or fumes. Send two people in opposite directions to call the emergency services if there is no phone nearby.

When you call the emergency services you will be asked:

- where you are
- how serious the collision is
- how many people or vehicles are involved
- whether anyone is seriously injured.

It is useful to assess where you are before you make this call, especially if you are on a motorway. On some occasions, passengers or witnesses will have to make these calls, if the driver or drivers involved are injured or in shock. All road users need to be prepared for this type of situation. It is important to remain calm at all times and to explain clearly what has happened. Once the call has been made, the operator will assess which emergency services are needed and the appropriate services will arrive at the scene of the accident as quickly as possible.

## How to deal with uninjured people

At the scene of the accident, you will need to consider the safety of others. Check for hazards such as fuel leakage, chemicals and broken glass. At this stage, it is important to guide the uninjured passengers to a safe place, away from the accident scene. This needs to be done with care, as some people may be in shock and not be able to assess the road conditions or their own injuries as accurately as they otherwise would have done.

**Key safety information**

- Always stay calm at the scene of an accident.
- Remember, emergency services can be contacted by ringing 999 or 112.
- Think carefully about the safety of other road users as well as your own if you are involved in a road traffic accident.

## Activity: Making that call

Select a partner and role-play a call to the emergency services.

- Imagine you are at the scene of a motorway road traffic accident. Two cars have collided and there are injuries.
- Before you start, decide what information will need to be passed on to the emergency services and the questions they might ask you.

**Just checking**

1 Identify four questions you are likely to be asked by the emergency services if you are required to call them from the scene of an accident.

2 What factors do you need to consider carefully before deciding to leave a vehicle or move other passengers from a vehicle after a road traffic accident?

3 Why is it important to report accidents to the police for your own insurance purposes?

# Legal requirements when involved in accidents

In this topic, you will learn about the different legal requirements that you must follow if you are involved in a road traffic accident. It is important that all road users know how to handle the situation if they are involved in an accident. If the driver of a vehicle is in shock, it may be important for a friend and/or passenger to remind the driver of the correct legal procedure to follow.

## Activity: Hit from behind

Mehul was driving to work as usual when another vehicle ran into his car from behind as he slowed at a junction. The accident happened at a slow speed and there was only slight damage to the vehicles; both drivers stopped at the scene.

1 What information will Mehul need to give to the other driver?

2 The other driver has admitted that it was her fault. Does Mehul need to tell his insurance company about the incident?

3 Will the incident need to be reported to the police?

## Duty of care

As a road user you have what is known as a 'duty of care' in relation to all other road users. This means that you must not put other road users at undue risk through your own behaviour while using the road. It is important to drive safely and to ensure that the vehicle being used is in roadworthy condition. All motor vehicles over three years old are required to have an annual MOT check to ensure that they are roadworthy. It is illegal to drive a vehicle of this age without an MOT certificate.

### Key terms

Duty of care – a legal obligation to maintain a reasonable standard of care when using the roads and maintaining a road vehicle.

MOT – a certificate showing that a vehicle has passed its roadworthiness check.

# Legal requirements if you are involved in a motor vehicle accident

If you are involved in a road accident, it is important to know what information you need to give to other parties involved, what details these people are entitled to know and what information needs to be given to the police and to your insurance company.

**Did you know?**

Bicycle riders do not need to have insurance, but if they are involved in an accident they may be able to claim compensation through their household insurance.

| Action needed | What you are legally required to do | When you need to complete this action by |
|---|---|---|
| Deal with the accident and talk to any other parties involved. For example, if you drive into another person's garden wall, you will need to discuss this with them as you are responsible for the damage. | Stop at the scene of the accident for a reasonable amount of time. Make contact with any other people involved. | Immediately |
| Provide basic details to the other party or parties involved in the accident. | Give your name, address, vehicle registration number and details of the vehicle's owner if this is not you. If anybody is injured, you will also need to exchange insurance details. If you do not have the insurance certificate with you, details need to be exchanged within 24 hours. | At the scene of the accident or ASAP or to the police within 24 hours |
| Report to the police | Report the accident to the police. You will need to take with you your driving licence, insurance documents, vehicle log and – if your car is over three years old – your MOT certificate. You will be issued with an accident number, which you will need to use in your dealings with your insurance company. | ASAP or within 7 days |
| Report to your insurance company | All accidents need to be reported to your insurance company even if you are not making a claim and are not at fault in causing the accident. | ASAP |

## Activity: Document log

Create a paper document log of all relevant legal details, which you can keep with you in your vehicle and which you might need if you are involved in an accident.

This log will need to include your:

- driving licence number
- insurance company and policy number
- vehicle registration number
- MOT number
- personal address and telephone number.

# Consequences of failing to stop after an accident

If you do not stop at the scene of an accident and report the accident you will be committing two road traffic offences:

1 Failure to stop at an accident

2 Failure to report an accident.

There are penalties for both offences. These can be fines and/or points on your driving licence. A court could also disqualify you from driving for one or both of these offences.

# What to do if you run over an animal

If you run over a dog, horse, cow, ass, mule, sheep, pig or goat, the Road Traffic Act 1988 requires that you stop and report the accident to the police. The police may ask for your details and you may need to show your insurance papers. The police will help to warn other drivers of any obstructions and arrange for the road to be cleared.

If you hit an animal that is not on this list, such as a cat, there are no legal requirements. However, there are things you can do to help ensure the safety of other road users and to get the appropriate care for the animal.

If the animal is injured and needs medical attention, you can call the RSPCA who will send an inspector to the scene. If you run over a dog, you can also call your local dog warden. Your local council will be able to give you the correct contact details.

---

**Key safety information**

- Always stop at the scene of an accident.

- Ensure that any vehicle on the road is roadworthy and does not put other road users at risk.

---

**Just checking**

1 Identify four documents you will need to present to the police if you are involved in a road traffic accident.

2 What action are you legally required to take if you kill or injure a cat or dog while using the road?

3 Why is it important for passengers to know the legal requirements of a driver if a road accident occurs?

# First aid at accident scenes

In this topic, you will learn about the basic first aid procedures that may be useful to know at the scene of an accident. About 55 per cent of deaths in road traffic accidents occur within the first few minutes after the accident, and 85 per cent of these people would have survived if first aid had been administered promptly.

## How to respond at the scene of an accident

The actions you take at the scene of an accident may mean the difference between life and death, even if you have no formal training.

The biggest immediate risks are that other vehicles may become involved in further collisions or that a fire may break out. Approach all the vehicles with care and ensure their engines are switched off. Try to make other road users aware of the danger and ensure that nobody smokes at the scene, as this will be a major fire hazard. Make sure the emergency services are contacted and let them know the exact location and the number of vehicles involved. If there are other people at the scene, get them to help if they can.

## What not to do

There is a temptation to try to do too much at the scene of the accident, but you should try to wait for the arrival of the emergency services. It is best to leave casualties where they are, so that specially trained people can deal with each injured person in the most appropriate manner. However, if anyone is at further risk – for instance, if it looks like a fire is developing – you will need to make a judgement and move casualties if necessary. If a motorcyclist is involved in an accident, do not remove their helmet unless you really have to.

## Symptoms of shock and how to respond

Being involved in an accident can be a real shock for many people. Look out for the common symptoms of shock. These may include:

- feeling faint or sick
- feeling dizzy
- breathing becoming rapid or shallow
- skin feeling cold and clammy.

If someone is showing these symptoms, try to make them warm and comfortable. Reassure them that help is on the way and do not leave them alone. Avoid unnecessary movement and

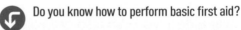

Do you know how to perform basic first aid?

help them to remain calm. If they are able to move, make sure they do not put themselves at risk by wandering back on to the roads as their judgement may be impaired at this time.

## Providing emergency care

To provide emergency care it is important to remember the mnemonic **DRABC**:

| Letter | Meaning |
|--------|---------|
| D | Danger – check that you are not in danger |
| R | Response – try to get a response from the casualty by speaking to them and gently shaking their shoulders |
| A | Airway – check the airways of the casualty are clear and kept open so they can breathe. Tilt the head backwards gently |
| B | Breathing – check for normal breathing. When the airways are open, this should happen automatically but check carefully for the first ten seconds |
| C | Compression – if the casualty is not breathing, compressions to the chest will need to be administered to maintain the circulation of oxygen in the blood. This is done by placing two hands on the centre of the chest and pressing down about 4 to 5 cm at a rate of about 100 compressions per minute. Use only one hand for a child<br><br>Then tilt the casualty's head backwards, pinch the nostrils of the nose gently and place your mouth over theirs. Give two breaths, each one lasting one second. Check if breathing has started and, if not, continue until the emergency services arrive |

## How to deal with bleeding

If one or more of the casualties is bleeding, it may be necessary for you to take action before the emergency services arrive. Check to see if there is anything in the wound such as glass. If there is nothing embedded in the wound, apply some firm pressure; however, if there is an object there, take care not to press on it. Fasten a pad to the wound and secure this with a bandage or length of cloth. Use the cleanest materials you have available at the time. If a limb is bleeding but is not broken, raise it to a level above the heart, as this reduces the flow of blood.

**Key safety information**

- Always ensure your own safety before starting to handle accident situations.

- Make the accident scene safe for other road users.

- Do not remove helmets from motorcyclists unless you have to.

## Dealing with burns

If a casualty at an accident has experienced burns, try to cool the burns by running them under clean cold water. You may use other similar liquids, but make sure they are **non-toxic**. Do not try to remove anything sticking to the wound, as this may be protecting the site of the injury and could need specialist attention.

**Just checking**

1  What would be the first actions you would take if you were the first to arrive at a road traffic accident?
2  How many compressions per minute should you do if you are trying to re-start someone's breathing?
3  What symptoms would you look for to assess whether a road traffic accident victim was suffering from shock?

# Assessment overview

While working through this unit, you will have prepared for the following assessment tasks:

| 1.1 | Identify the checks and maintenance that should be carried out regularly on a form of transport | Pages 24–35 |
|---|---|---|
| 1.2 | State why regular checks are important | Pages 24–35 |
| 2.1 | Carry out safety checks on a form of transport | Pages 36–37 |
| 3.1 | Describe what to do if you are in a vehicle that breaks down | Pages 38–40 |
| 3.2 | Describe what to do if you are involved in or witness an accident | Pages 41–45 |
| 3.3 | Identify appropriate responses to situations requiring first aid | Pages 46–47 |

edexcel

advancing learning, changing lives

# Assignment tips

➔ **Task 1.** To meet assessment criteria 1.1 and 1.2, you will need to identify checks and maintenance that should be carried out on a form of transport. You will then need to state why these regular checks are necessary. This must relate to one type of wheeled vehicle.

➔ **Task 2.** To meet assessment criteria 2.1, you will need to carry out safety checks on one type of wheeled transport. It would make good sense to combine Tasks 1 and 2 and complete them at one time. You could explain to a tutor the checks that are needed on a type of wheeled vehicle, demonstrate these checks to your tutor and then state why each check is important.

➔ **Task 3.** To meet assessment criteria 3.1, 3.2 and 3.3, you will need to;

- describe what to do when you are in a vehicle that breaks down

- describe what to do when you are in a vehicle involved in an accident or you witness an accident

- identify appropriate responses to situations that require first aid.

You could complete this task through role plays, with your tutor asking questions, or through written scenarios which your tutor presents to you. The assessment evidence for this task could also involve you answering structured multiple-choice questions or short-answer questions set by your tutor.

# Knowing the rules of the road

In this unit, you will develop your knowledge and understanding of how to stay safe when using the road. By the end of this unit, you will understand why all road users need to remain focused at all times, considering their own safety and the safety of other people on the roads. You will also learn the meanings of different road signs and symbols, and learn to understand the signals given by other people, such as the police. Finally, you will find out about the correct procedures to follow at level crossings or tramways.

After completing this unit, you should:

- have developed your knowledge of how pedestrians can use the roads safely
- know the rules and responsibilities cyclists, motorcyclists and learner drivers have when using the roads
- know traffic signs giving orders
- know traffic signs giving warnings and directions
- know requirements for road users related to lights and signals
- know how road users can stay safe in relation to tramways and level crossings.

This unit could be integrated with or reinforced by other units. It may be useful to refer to the relevant sections in units 1, 2 and 4.

## Do you know the rules?

Your local college is running a four-week evening course for young people, to help them develop their road safety skills. The course is sponsored by the local council, which is concerned about the safety of new drivers. Over the past five years, there have been a number of fatal accidents in the area, many of them involving young, newly qualified drivers.

The course covers all aspects of road safety, but Week 3 focuses on 'knowing the rules of the road'. Tom, Sarah and Jessica are working together to research the different types of signs and signals that road users need to be aware of. They are also developing their general knowledge about how road users can stay safe on the road.

The group has been asked to think about the following questions.

### Thinking points

- ➔ How are road signs giving orders different from road signs giving warnings?

- ➔ What problems may arise if a road user ignores signs giving orders?

- ➔ Why is it important that all pedestrians follow the Green Cross Code when crossing the road?

- ➔ Describe the types of clothing cyclists should wear to make themselves more visible to other road users.

- ➔ Why should cyclists always dismount at level crossings and tramways?

# General guidance for pedestrians [HC Rules 1–7]

In this topic, you will learn about the general rules that pedestrians need to follow to make sure they stay safe when using the roads. As a pedestrian, you must know where and how to cross the road as safely as possible. You should also make sure that you can be seen clearly by other road users in different weather conditions and at different times of the day.

## Where to walk

Pedestrians should always walk on the **pavement** if there is one, and keep well away from the kerb where possible. Vehicles may occasionally mount the pavement or kerb by accident, so you should try to avoid walking at the edge of the pavement with your back to oncoming traffic.

When crossing the road, you must always look both ways before stepping into the road. Many people are injured or killed each year because they have run out into the road without looking. Children and adolescents are especially at risk, because they may be distracted by their friends and sometimes do not appreciate the speed of traffic using the road.

If there is no pavement, you should walk on the right-hand side of the road so that you can see any oncoming traffic. However, if there is a sharp right-hand bend, you should cross to the other side of the road so that oncoming traffic can see you more easily. Cross back to the right-hand side of the road once you have passed the bend.

Where there is no pavement, groups of people should walk in single file and keep as close to the side of the road as possible. This will reduce the risk of accidents.

## Being seen as a pedestrian

Your safety on the roads depends to a large extent on whether other road users can see you, so, as a pedestrian, you should wear clothes that make you more visible. In low light conditions, wear light-coloured or fluorescent clothing. In the dark, make sure you wear something reflective which will be very visible in a vehicle's headlights. You can choose from a wide range of reflective garments, including:

- fluorescent waistcoats, jackets or tabards
- fluorescent or reflective armbands or sashes
- trainers or jogging trousers with reflective strips or patches.

> **Key term**
>
> **Pavement** – a specially designed space at the side of a road, where pedestrians can walk safely.

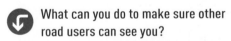
What can you do to make sure other road users can see you?

## Activity: Goole Striders

The athletics club in Goole has a reputation for long-distance running. In the winter, members of the club do a lot of road running and often use country roads that have no pavements. These runs usually start at 7 pm.

- Design a leaflet which can be given to all club members. The leaflet should give advice and guidance about how to run safely on roads in winter.

### Key safety information

- Always walk on the pavement if there is one.
- Never walk on a motorway or a slip road to a motorway.
- Wear bright or fluorescent clothing to make yourself more visible to other road users.
- Learn and follow the Green Cross Code when crossing the road.

## The Green Cross Code

All children should be taught the **Green Cross Code** by their parents or carers and all pedestrians – however old or young – should follow the code at all times. The five key points of the Green Cross Code are:

- Find a safe place to cross.
- Stop just before you get to the kerb.
- Look all around for traffic and listen.
- If traffic is coming, let it pass.
- When safe, go straight across the road – but do not run.

### Key term

**Green Cross Code** – a set of instructions which tells pedestrians how to cross the road safely.

## Activity: Green Cross Code

1 Find a copy of the Highway Code and look carefully at the section covering the Green Cross Code.

2 Design a poster, including all five 'tag lines', which gives more detail about how to follow the code and stay safe.

### Just checking

1 Why are children and older adults particularly at risk when crossing the road?

2 Why might pedestrians be more at risk in winter?

# Being a safe pedestrian in unusual situations [HC Rules 8–26 and 28–35]

In this topic, you will learn about some of the situations where pedestrians need to take particular care to ensure their safety on the road. You will learn to avoid many everyday hazards by following some general road safety principles.

## Taking particular care

| Safety issue for the pedestrian | Possible dangers | Actions which may help |
|---|---|---|
| Crossing side roads | Not seeing traffic<br><br>Rear wheels of articulated lorries mounting the pavement as they negotiate a turn | Look behind you before stepping into the road, and look out for traffic turning into the side road |
| Pedestrian safety barriers | Ignoring the designated crossing point and crossing somewhere more risky<br><br>Jumping over the barriers | Only cross the road where there are gaps in the barriers<br><br>Never climb barriers or walk between them |
| One-way streets | Not noticing the direction of traffic<br><br>Not realising that traffic in bus or cycle lanes may go in the opposite direction | Check which way traffic is moving<br><br>Look out for bus and cycle lanes |
| Bus and cycle lanes | Buses and bicycles may be moving faster than the traffic in the main highway | Always check the speed of vehicles in bus or cycle lanes |
| Parked vehicles | Pedestrians are not able to see clearly<br><br>Vehicles are not able to see pedestrians | Avoid crossing the road near or between parked vehicles if possible<br><br>If you must cross between parked vehicles, treat the outside of the vehicles as the kerb of the road |
| Reversing vehicles | Driver of reversing vehicle may not see pedestrians | Never cross behind a vehicle that is reversing or about to reverse (check whether the white reversing lights are on) |
| Moving vehicles | Trying to jump into a moving vehicle<br><br>Drivers may not see pedestrians | Never try to get into or hold on to a moving vehicle<br><br>Let moving vehicles pass before trying to cross the road |

Who has right of way in this situation?

## Using road crossings safely

There are many different types of pedestrian crossing. Always cross the road at a designated crossing if possible, and make sure that all traffic has stopped before you start to cross the road.

You may have used the following types of crossing:

- traffic lights
- zebra crossings
- pelican crossings
- puffin crossings
- toucan crossings.

## Activity: Types of pedestrian crossing

1 Find a copy of the Highway Code and read about the different types of crossing listed above.

2 Create an information sheet for pedestrians, explaining how to use each of these crossings.

## Situations needing extra care

As a pedestrian, you must pay attention to emergency vehicles. If you see the flashing lights or hear the siren of an emergency vehicle, you must stay out of the road, even if you are at a pedestrian crossing and it is your turn to cross. You must also be aware that other vehicles may pull in to the side of the road to let the emergency vehicle pass. This may put you at risk.

When getting off a bus, wait until the bus has come to a complete stop before stepping out and look out for cyclists who may be coming up the inside of the bus or cycling on the pavement. If you need to cross the road, wait until the bus has left and you can see clearly in both directions. Never cross the road directly in front of or behind a bus.

As a pedestrian, you must also be aware of street and pavement repairs. Look out for signs or other obstacles on the pavement and take extra care if the pavement is closed and you have to walk into the road area or cross to the other side of the road.

Railway level crossings and tramways can be very dangerous to pedestrians, so you must take extra care if you come across either of them. These hazards are covered in more detail on pages 71–73.

 What rules should you follow when using a pedestrian crossing?

**Key safety information**

- Always pay attention to your surroundings.

- Take care around parked vehicles. They may be about to move off or reverse.

- When getting off a bus, never cross the road until the bus has left and you can see clearly in both directions.

---

### Just checking

1 How are pelican crossings different from puffin crossings?

2 What particular challenges do toucan crossings present to pedestrians?

3 If you need to cross a main road but there is no specific crossing, you should cross at a point where there is an island in the middle of the road. Why?

# Cyclists and staying safe [HC Rules 59–81]

In this topic, you will learn about some of the situations in which cyclists must take particular care when using the road. Cyclists are far more vulnerable than car drivers if they are involved in a road traffic accident, and other road users may not see cyclists or be aware of the risks.

## Clothing and bicycles

Cyclists are often difficult to see, especially in low light conditions or when the weather is bad. When you are cycling, it is very important to wear appropriate clothing and make yourself visible to other road users.

You should wear:

- a helmet
- visible (preferably **fluorescent** or **reflective**) clothing
- clothing which is appropriate for cycling (e.g. nothing which could get caught in the chain of your cycle).

At night, you must make sure your bicycle is fitted with:

- a white front light
- a red rear light
- a red rear reflector.

 Why is it so important for cyclists to make themselves visible to other road users?

### Key terms

**Fluorescent clothing** – clothing which is highly visible in poor light.

**Reflective clothing and accessories** – clothing and accessories which reflect light and help other road users to see you when it is dark.

## Activity: Clothing safety

Work with another person to create a table which describes:

- the different types of protective clothing available to cyclists
- how each of these items will help to increase the safety of the cyclist.

## Cycling safely

It is important to follow the Highway Code when cycling. Many of these rules are common sense – for example, do not ride a bicycle under the influence of alcohol or drugs. However, many cyclists are injured or killed each year because they have not followed basic safety rules.

The Highway Code rules for cyclists include:

- how to ride a bicycle safely
- how to use the road and be aware of other vehicles
- rules related to behaviour while riding a bicycle
- rules related to passengers.

## Activity: Ensuring safety on the roads

The Highway Code explains how cyclists should behave in certain situations. Find a copy of the Highway Code and use it to complete the table below. An example has been filled in for you.

| Highway Code Rule | How cyclists should respond to the rule |
|---|---|
| Using cycle tracks located away from the road (HC 62) | |
| Using cycle lanes along the carriageway (HC 63) | |
| Rules related to pavements (HC 64) | |
| Using bus lanes (HC 65) | Bus lanes can be used, but cyclists must look out for people getting on and off buses. Cyclists must take care when overtaking buses and must not ride between the kerb and the bus when the bus is parked. If these rules are not followed, there is an increased risk of accidents. |
| Cycling and staying safe (HC 66/67/68/69) | |
| Parking bicycles (HC 70) | |
| Traffic lights and bicycle safety (HC 71) | |

## Negotiating road junctions safely

As a cyclist, you must know the correct procedures to follow when turning left, turning right, riding on a dual carriageway and negotiating roundabouts. You must also pay particular attention to other vehicles at junctions. For example, if there is a side road on your left, you must be very careful not to cycle up the inside of vehicles which are indicating or slowing down to turn left.

## Activity: Junctions

Use the Highway Code to create a safety leaflet for children aged 8–10, explaining the rules cyclists must follow when:

- turning left
- turning right
- riding a bicycle on a dual carriageway
- going round a roundabout.

Use images and diagrams to make the leaflet easier for children to understand.

Are cyclists allowed to ride across this type of crossing?

## Crossing roads safely

When cycling, you must be aware of other road users, especially if you or they want to cross the road. This is for your own safety and the safety of other people. Toucan crossings are designed for both pedestrians and cyclists, and you are allowed to ride across these crossings. Other crossings are designed for cyclists only. At these crossings, you must wait until the green cycle symbol is showing before riding across.

At all other crossings, you must dismount and wheel your bicycle across the road. As a cyclist, you are not allowed to use equestrian crossings at all, as these crossings are designed specifically for horses.

You must take particular care at railway level crossings and tramways. You will often be instructed to dismount – there will be a 'cyclists dismount' sign. However, it is a good idea to walk even if you do not see one of these signs, especially if the rails are wet and slippery.

 **Key safety information**

- Learn how to ride a bicycle properly and practise turning left and right on and off roads.
- Always follow the Highway Code.
- Never cycle at night without proper bicycle lights and appropriate clothing.

---

**Just checking**

1. Why is it important to keep your hands on the handlebars at all times when cycling, unless you are signalling or changing gear?
2. Why is it advisable to have a bell fitted to your bicycle? When might you use your bell?
3. What might happen if you hold on to a moving motor vehicle when cycling?

# Motorcyclists and staying safe

In this topic, you will learn about some of the situations in which motorcyclists need to take particular care. Motorcyclists may appear to be more protected than cyclists, since their clothing seems to offer more protection. However, motorcyclists travel at very high speeds, which puts them at greater risk if they are involved in an accident.

## Wearing a helmet

Anyone riding a motorcycle, scooter or moped – including pillion passengers – must wear a securely fastened protective helmet. The only people who do not have to follow this rule are members of the Sikh religion who are wearing a turban. If you ride a motorcycle, you should check your helmet before every journey to make sure it is clean and in good condition. Check the manufacturer's instructions to ensure you are using a suitable cleaning product.

Riders of tricycles and quadricycles should also wear a helmet.

## Carrying passengers

The Highway Code has clear rules about motorcyclists carrying passengers, including:

- Motorcyclists can only carry one passenger.
- Passengers must sit astride the motorcycle on a proper seat.
- Passengers must face forward and have both feet on the footrests.
- Motorcyclists must only carry a passenger if the motorcycle is designed for that purpose.
- Provisional licence holders are not allowed to carry a pillion passenger.

 **Activity: Give me a lift!**

Amir has recently passed his motorcycle driving test. As he is leaving work, a friend asks him for a lift home. Amir agrees.

1 Work with a partner to role-play the conversation Amir will need to have with his friend before he gives him a lift.

2 His friend has never been on a motorcycle. What safety information will Amir need to give his friend?

## Advanced stop lines

At some signal-controlled junctions, you will see **advanced stop lines**. These allow cyclists to wait ahead of the other traffic at the junction, which increases their safety when the traffic begins to move again.

Motorcyclists, like motorists, must stop at the first white line if the lights are amber or red. When riding a motorcycle, you must avoid blocking the marked area. However, if the lights turn red after you have crossed the first stop line, you must stop at the second white line, even if this means stopping in the marked area.

When the lights turn green, give cyclists the time and space they need to move off safely. By following this procedure, you will reduce the chances of an accident.

## Riding in windy or hot weather

You must take extra care when riding a motorcycle or moped in windy conditions. You may be blown off course by strong gusts of wind, so you should keep your distance from other vehicles and allow plenty of space when overtaking. Other vehicles – especially tall vehicles, such as lorries – may also be affected, so you will need to pay close attention to the vehicles around you.

Hot and sunny weather may cause various problems for motor-cyclists. For your own safety, you must be aware of these hazards.

- You may become drowsy in the heat. If you notice your attention wandering, pull over and take a break.

- The road surface may become soft in high temperatures, which will affect braking and steering. You must be aware of these changes and adjust your riding appropriately.

- On a bright sunny day, you are more likely to be dazzled by the sunlight. If you are finding it difficult to see, you will need to slow down or even stop. In these conditions, it is even more important that your visor is clean.

 Why are advanced stop lines used at some junctions?

### Key term

**Advanced stop line** – a protected area for cyclists at some road junctions.

### Key safety information

- Always wear a safety helmet when riding a motorbike, moped or scooter.

- Take extra care when riding in windy conditions, and observe how other vehicles are being affected by the wind. Your life may depend on it!

- If you are carrying a passenger, always make sure that they follow the correct safety procedures.

### Just checking

1  What are the advantages for cyclists and motorcyclists of the advanced stop lines at some road junctions?
2  Not all countries have the same rules about wearing a helmet when riding a motorcycle. Why is it important for your own safety to follow UK rules, even when you are abroad?

# Horse riders and staying safe [HC Rules 49–55]

Visibility and well-maintained tack are important for rider safety

In this topic, you will learn about the Highway Code rules that apply to horse riders. Many road users do not know how to approach or pass a horse and rider safely. It is the rider's responsibility to ensure that they and their horse can be seen clearly, and that the horse is safe to be on the road. Remember that a horse is not a machine and may react in unexpected ways, especially if startled.

## Safety equipment and clothing

When riding a horse, you must make sure your head is protected. It is advisable for all riders to wear a helmet, and children under the age of 14 must wear a securely fastened helmet by law. (Sikh children wearing a turban do not have to follow this law.)

It is important that all riders wear:

- boots or shoes with hard soles and heels
- reflective clothing at night or when visibility is poor
- light-coloured or fluorescent clothing in daylight.

These actions will increase the safety of the rider and the road users around them.

You should avoid riding a horse on the road at night or when visibility is poor. If you do have to ride a horse at night, make sure you are wearing reflective clothing and that your horse is wearing **reflective fetlock bands** and a **reflective tail guard**. You should also wear a light which shows white to the front and red to the rear. This can be worn on a band around your arm or leg/boot.

If you are leading a horse along a road in the dark, you must carry a light in your right hand, which shows white to the front and red to the rear. You must also make sure that you and your horse are wearing reflective clothing.

### Key terms

**Reflective fetlock bands** – reflective bands worn around a horse's fetlocks when it is dark, so that the horse can be seen more easily by other road users.

**Reflective/fluorescent tail guard** – a guard which should be worn around a horse's tail at night to make the horse more visible.

## Activity: Rider clothing and safety

1 Use the Internet to research the number of accidents involving horse riders in a typical year in the UK.

2 What type of injuries are suffered during these accidents?

## Horse riding

Before taking a horse onto the road, you must make sure that:

- the tack fits and is in good condition
- the horse can be kept under control.

You should never ride a horse without a saddle or bridle, as this will put you and other road users at risk.

Nervous horses should never be ridden alone on the road. However, a nervous horse can be made more comfortable if it is part of a group of less nervous horses.

## Activity: Rules for riding horses on the road (HC Rule 53)

1 Use the Highway Code to find out more about the general rules that horse riders are expected to follow when riding on the roads.

2 Produce a poster which outlines these rules.

## Roundabouts

If you are riding a horse, you should avoid roundabouts wherever possible because they are difficult to negotiate safely on a horse. If you cannot avoid going round a roundabout, you should:

- keep to the left
- watch out for vehicles crossing your path as they join or leave the roundabout
- signal right when crossing an exit, to show that you are not intending to leave the roundabout
- signal left just before leaving the roundabout.

If you follow these rules, you will be able to show other road users what you are planning to do and reduce the risk of accidents.

**Key safety information**

- Always wear light-coloured or fluorescent clothing when riding a horse on the road.
- Avoid riding a horse on the road in conditions where visibility is poor.
- Never ride a nervous horse on the road.
- Avoid riding a horse on the road when it is dark.

### Just checking

1 Why is it important for a rider to keep both hands on the reins and both feet in the stirrups when riding a horse?

2 Why is it better to ride horses in single file on narrow roads?

3 Highway Code Rule 54 states that horse riders must not take a horse onto a pavement, footpath or cycle track. Why is this rule so important in ensuring the safety of riders, pedestrians and cyclists?

# Traffic signs giving orders [HC Rules, pages 106–107]

In this topic, you will learn about the different types of road traffic sign that give orders. You will need to recognise and know the meaning of all these signs in order to complete the test for this unit.

## Traffic signs giving orders

Traffic signs giving orders are usually circular, with a red border or background. These signs are often prohibitive (that is, they tell you things you cannot do). The orders given by these signs are intended to increase the safety of all road users, so it is very important that you follow them. Any road user who ignores an order given by a traffic sign can be prosecuted and punished for doing so. For example, if you break the speed limit you can be fined and/or have penalty points added to your driving licence.

Traffic signs giving orders may have instructions written below them, to help road users understand what they mean.

Maximum speed

No entry for vehicular traffic

No cycling

No motor vehicles

No overtaking

No U-turns

## Activity: Know your traffic signs

1 Find a copy of the Highway Code and look at the section titled 'Signs giving orders'.

2 Create an information sheet which explains what these signs mean. Make sure you cover all the signs in this section: you will need to recognise them in order to pass your driving theory test.

# Traffic signs giving instructions

Traffic signs giving instructions are almost always blue and usually circular. These signs do not have a red border, since this would show that they were giving orders. These signs may have a message written below them, to help road users understand what they mean.

Ahead only

Minimum speed

Segregated pedal cycle and pedestrian route

Turn left ahead

With-flow bus and cycle lane

Route to be used by pedal cycles only

## Activity: Signs giving instructions

1 Find a copy of the Highway Code and look at the section titled 'Signs with blue circles but no red border mostly give positive instruction'.

2 Working with a partner, write some multiple-choice questions to test your knowledge of these signs. Make sure you cover all the signs in this section as you will need to know about them to pass the test for this unit or your driving theory test.

# How signs giving orders are different from other signs

Signs giving orders are different from those giving positive instructions. Signs giving orders usually have a red edge and a white background.

Signs giving warnings are different again: these signs are usually triangular with a red edge.

## Signs used by school crossing patrols

Children arriving at or leaving school are often distracted by their friends and may step into the road without warning or try to cross when it is not safe to do so. This is why **school crossing patrol personnel** are employed. They have the authority to tell other road users to stop, so that children can cross the road safely.

**Key term**

**School crossing patrol personnel** – people who work at school entrances and help children to cross the road safely.

## Activity: A school crossing patrol

1 Find a copy of the Highway Code and look at the section titled 'Signals by authorised persons'.

2 Find the page about school crossing personnel. Learn these signals and make sure you can recognise them and understand what they mean.

**Key safety information**

- Always follow signs giving instructions
- Make sure you read any additional information with a sign. This will make the instructions clear.

**Just checking**

1 What are the potential consequences for a driver and for other road users if the driver ignores a 'no overtaking' sign?

2 What are the likely consequences if a driver parks in an 'urban clearway' area during a restricted time (e.g. 8.00 am–9.00 am)?

3 Why is it necessary to impose a speed limit of 20 miles per hour in some areas, to improve safety.

# Traffic signs giving warnings and directions [HC pages 108–109]

In this topic, you will learn about the different types of road traffic sign that give warnings to road users. Warning signs are very helpful, as they provide information that makes driving or riding safer. You will need to recognise and understand all the signs in the 'Warning signs' section of the Highway Code in order to complete the test for Unit 3 in the Certificate in Safe Road Skills.

## Traffic signs giving warnings

Warning signs are usually triangular in shape and are used to raise road users' awareness. For example, you may see signs warning that you are approaching a junction, a roundabout or a steep hill. In all these situations, you will need to take some form of action, such as slowing down or changing into a lower gear.

Warning signs may also provide information about unusual situations or events that road users should be aware of. For example, they may warn road users that the road surface is uneven or slippery, or that wild animals might roam into the road. Such warnings allow road users to react appropriately to any hazards they encounter, increasing their own safety and the safety of other people on the roads.

Dual carriageway ends

Junction on bend ahead

Roundabout

Uneven road

Opening or swing bridge ahead

Low-flying aircraft or sudden aircraft noise

Falling or fallen rocks

Slippery road

Steep hill downwards

Level crossing without barrier or gate ahead

Cycle route ahead

Wild animals

## Activity: Know your warning signs

1 Find a copy of the Highway Code and look at the section titled 'Warning signs'.

2 Create a set of flashcards, with one sign on each card.

3 Work with a partner and spend 20 minutes learning what the different warning signs mean. Then use the flashcards to test each other and make sure you both recognise and understand the signs.

Temporary warning signs may be placed at the side of the road to warn of unusual or short-lived conditions such as flooding or ice. These warnings help road users to drive or ride appropriately and increase their safety and the safety of people around them.

## How signs giving warnings are different from other signs

Signs giving warnings:

- are usually triangular in shape
- usually have a red border and a white background
- often have information written below the sign to help road users understand the warning.

### Key safety information

- Always pay attention to the information given by warning signs. These signs are there to increase your safety and the safety of other road users.

- React appropriately to any warning signs you see. The actions you take in response to these signs could save your life or the lives of other road users.

### Just checking

1 When driving a car, how should you react if you see a sign warning you that there is a right-hand bend coming up with a junction on the bend?

2 If you are riding a motor scooter, how should you respond to a sign warning that the road is slippery?

3 If you are driving a vehicle, how should you respond to a sign telling you that there is no footway for pedestrians for 400 yards?

# Traffic lights, flashing red lights and signals [HC Rules 103/105/210/218 and pages 102–103]

In this topic, you will learn:

* the meaning of traffic light signals road users need to understand
* the meaning of signals given by other road users as they drive or ride their vehicles
* the importance of responding quickly to emergency vehicles displaying flashing lights.

## Understanding general signals given by other road users

Drivers, motorcyclists, cyclists and horse riders need to give clear signals to other road users, to show their intentions. For example, if you are intending to stop, move off or change direction, you must tell other road users what you are about to do. This reduces the risk of accidents and increases your safety and the safety of those around you.

You may signal your intentions using lights or arm signals. Drivers and motorcyclists generally use lights, for example:

* red brake lights show that a vehicle is slowing down or stopping
* a white light at the back of a vehicle shows that it is reversing
* yellow flashing lights at the side of a vehicle show that the driver is intending to change direction.

Arm signals are most commonly used by cyclists or horse riders. However, they are also used to reinforce other indication signals, or if a vehicle's signalling system (for example, the indicator lights on a car) is not working.

### Activity: Understanding the arm signals of others

1 Find a copy of the Highway Code and look at the section titled 'Signals to other road users'. Do you recognise all of the arm signals shown?

2 Create an information sheet for learner drivers, which clearly shows and explains the meaning of the arm signals other road users may use.

All road users must obey any signals given by police officers, traffic officers, traffic wardens or school crossing patrol people. For example, if a school crossing patrol person is showing the 'Stop for children' sign, all road users must stop.

## Traffic light signals

Most road users are familiar with the sequence of traffic light signals, having seen and understood them since childhood. However, these signals are often ignored (for example, a motorist may ignore a red or amber traffic light) and many people are injured each year as a result.

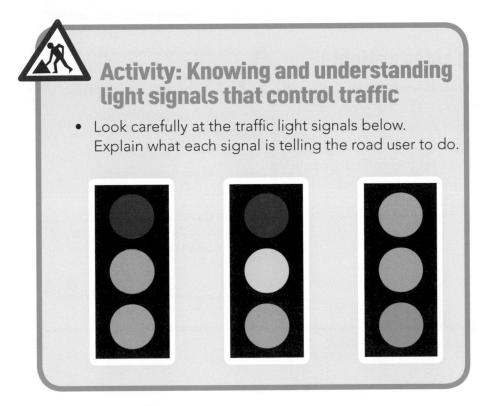

### Activity: Knowing and understanding light signals that control traffic

- Look carefully at the traffic light signals below. Explain what each signal is telling the road user to do.

## Understanding flashing red lights

As a road user, you will occasionally need to pass over level crossings. These crossings use light signals to show whether it is safe for you to carry on.

If the amber light comes on as you are crossing, you should carry on as normal. If you see amber or red lights as you are approaching the crossing, there may be a train approaching and you must stop. Never drive across a red light.

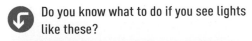
Do you know what to do if you see lights like these?

After the train has passed, wait until the lights have gone off before carrying on with your journey. If the lights carry on flashing, there may be another train approaching and you must wait.

## Activity: Flashing red lights

1 Find a copy of the Highway Code and look at the section titled 'Light signals controlling traffic'.

2 Where – apart from at a level crossing – might you see flashing red lights like this?

## Traffic incidents and warning signs or lights

Police officers and traffic officers frequently have to deal with accidents or other incidents on roads and motorways, and they often need to get to the scene of an accident or incident quickly. If you see the flashing red or blue lights of an emergency vehicle, you must slow down to let the vehicle pass. Many road users choose to pull over to give these vehicles more space.

### Key safety information

- Always respond to the traffic signals used by members of the emergency services.

- Never go through an amber traffic light.

- Always signal before moving out onto the road, so that other people know what you are intending to do.

### Just checking

1 Why is it important to signal clearly before changing lanes on the motorway?

2 Explain the possible consequences of trying to cross a level crossing when the traffic lights are showing amber or red.

# Safety at level crossings and tramways

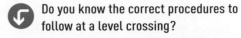
Do you know the correct procedures to follow at a level crossing?

In this topic, you will learn how to stay safe at level crossings and in areas where there are tramways. Accidents at level crossings are often fatal, because trains are extremely heavy and cannot slow down quickly, so you need to know the correct procedures to follow at these crossings.

In recent years, tramway systems have been reintroduced in some cities – Sheffield, for example – to ease congestion in city centres. However, many road users are unfamiliar with the procedures to follow around tramways. In this topic, you will learn how to drive or ride safely around trams.

## Information about level crossings [HC Rules 82/291/293/295–299]

A level crossing is where a road crosses a railway line or tramway line. All road users need to take extra care at level crossings and cyclists should dismount and wheel their cycles across. When you are approaching a level crossing in a vehicle, you must:

- approach and cross with care
- make sure the road is clear on the far side of the crossing before driving onto the crossing
- leave a reasonable distance between your vehicle and the vehicle in front of you
- never stop or park on or near a level crossing.

### Controlled level crossings

**Controlled level crossings** are the most common type of crossing. These crossings use traffic lights and sound to warn road users if there is a train coming, and they may have full- or half-length barriers as well.

When a train is approaching a controlled level crossing, a steady amber light will come on. This warns road users that the flashing red stop lights are about to come on and the barriers are about to come down (if there are any). When the red lights are flashing, an alarm will sound as well.

> **Key term**
>
> **Controlled level crossing** – a level crossing with traffic lights and barriers.

71

As a road user, you must:

- **always** obey the flashing red stop lights
- **always** stop behind the white lines on the road
- **keep going** if the amber lights come on after you have crossed the white lines
- **wait** if the red lights continue to flash after a train has passed. There will be another train coming
- **only** cross when the lights have gone off and the barriers have gone up
- **never** zigzag around half barriers
- **never** reverse onto or over a level crossing.

## Activity: Level crossing safety

1 Use the Internet to research the number of accidents and injuries that occur at controlled crossings each year in the UK.

2 Suggest some activities, which could be carried out with young people, to encourage safety at level crossings.

## Other types of level crossing

There are three different types of level crossing:

- level crossings without traffic lights
- level crossings with user-operated gates or barriers
- **open level crossings**.

As a road user, you will need to know the correct procedures to follow at each type of crossing.

### Key term

**Open level crossing** – a level crossing with no gates, barriers, traffic lights or attendants.

## Activity: Different types of level crossing

1 Find a copy of the Highway Code and look at Rules 293–299.

2 Create a poster explaining the correct procedure to follow at each type of crossing and the safety issues road users should be aware of.

## Incidents and breakdowns at crossings

If you break down, or are involved in an accident or other incident at a level crossing, you must follow the correct procedure.

- Get everyone out of the vehicle and clear of the level crossing immediately.

- Use the railway telephone (if there is one) to contact the signal operator. There will be clear instructions on the telephone, explaining what to do and what you need to tell the signal operator.
- Move the vehicle off the crossing if there is time. However, if the amber or red warning lights come on, you must leave the vehicle and move away from the crossing.

## Information about tramways [HC Rules 82/300/301/305/306]

You will need to take extra care in areas with tramways, because trams are wider than other vehicles and may not follow the same rules as other road users. Never enter a road, lane or other route reserved for trams.

You must always give priority to trams, especially when they are moving away from tram stops. This is very important because trams are often carrying large numbers of people who could be injured if the tram has to make an emergency stop.

If you are following a tram, you must not try to overtake or pass on the inside. You may overtake when the tram stops for passengers (as long as it is safe to do so), but you must look out for passengers who have just got off the tram.

Trams may be allowed to drive into areas where other traffic is not permitted – for example, a tram route may go down a road which is closed to cars during rush hour. There will be signs to show which road vehicles can use these routes and at what times of day. If you ignore these signs and use a tram lane when you are not supposed to, you may be prosecuted, fined and receive penalty points on your driving licence.

You should avoid driving or riding directly on the tram rails, especially at bends and junctions where tracks change direction. This is particularly important for cyclists, since a bicycle tyre is narrow enough to become trapped in a tram rail. If you are cycling or riding a motorcycle, try to cross the tracks at right angles for safety. Other road users should give cyclists and motorcyclists more space to do this.

 Are there any tramways in your local area?

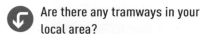

### Key safety information

- Always follow the correct procedure at level crossings.
- Never pass through a red or amber flashing light at a level crossing.
- Give trams plenty of space and look out for passengers at tram stops.

### Just checking

1 Why is it important that all road users know the rules related to level crossing safety?
2 What reasons do you think members of the public give for ignoring the Highway Code rules related to level crossings?

# Assessment overview

While working through this unit, you will have prepared for the following assessment tasks:

| | | |
|---|---|---|
| 1.1 | Identify requirements of the Highway Code for pedestrians | Pages 51–55 |
| 1.2 | Identify requirements of the Highway Code in relation to vulnerable vehicle users | Pages 56–62 |
| 2.1 | Interpret traffic signs giving orders | Pages 63–65 |
| 2.2 | Interpret traffic signs giving warnings and directions | Pages 66–67 |
| 2.3 | Identify the requirements related to lights and signals | Pages 68–70 |
| 3.1 | Identify requirements of the Highway Code relating to level crossings and tramways | Pages 71–73 |

## Assignment tips

This unit will be assessed using an online multiple-choice test that is externally set and externally marked. There will be 20 questions in this test and you will need to achieve a score of 17 in order to pass.

You can practise for this test by working through the bank of multiple-choice questions provided by the examining board. You will also benefit from studying the official Highway Code, in hard copy or online.

Once you have gained the 13-credit Edexcel Level 1 Certificate in Safe Road Skills and Attitudes, you will be eligible to sit a shorter version of the theory test for drivers, known as the Abridged Theory Test. You must take this theory test within three years of the date on your qualification certificate.

# Recognising safe road use

This unit promotes safety for road users and passengers of all forms of transport. In this unit, you will gain an understanding of the impact that your attitudes and behaviours can have on other road users.

After completing this unit, you should:

- know the types of vulnerable road user
- know different methods of traffic calming
- know how behaviour and attitudes affect other road users.

**CASE STUDY**

# Party time!

Tom, Atique and Meeta are travelling to a friend's 18th birthday party in the centre of Carlisle. It is 10.00 pm and they are already late – the party started at 8.00 pm. It is a lovely warm summer's evening and everybody is in a good mood.

Tom and Meeta are travelling together by car. Atique is following on his moped. They are looking forward to the evening and Tom is playing his favourite dance music loudly, with the car windows open.

Tom is on his mobile phone, chatting to a friend as he drives; Meeta is also on the phone, trying to get directions to the party. She gives directions to Tom when she can and also passes them on to Atique using hand signals through the back window of the car.

When the roads are clear, or if they are on a dual carriageway, Atique often speeds up to drive alongside the car, to chat to Tom and check on directions. He has no idea where the party is, so he is just following the car as best he can.

## Thinking points

→ What sorts of behaviour are Tom, Atique and Meeta displaying which may mean that Tom is distracted from his driving?

→ How are Tom, Meeta and Atique placing themselves – and other road users – at risk?

→ Why is Atique's behaviour so difficult for other road users to deal with?

→ If you were a passenger in the car with Tom and Meeta, what actions would you take to improve the group's safety?

→ What should Tom, Meeta and Atique have done earlier in the evening to increase their own and other road users' safety?

# Vulnerable road users

In this topic, you will learn about the different types of **vulnerable road user**, such as young children riding bicycles and older people trying to cross busy roads. These people will need to be treated with particular care by other road users, and they also need to be aware of the risks they face when completing journeys and the ways in which they can reduce these risks.

There are many different methods of transport which you can use to complete journeys (see Unit 1). The method you choose, and the obstacles you encounter on your journey, are the main factors which affect your vulnerability on the roads.

## Pedestrians

People who complete journeys on foot may face a number of challenges. Pavements are often in poor condition and you may trip or fall, causing yourself injury. In some places, pavements may not exist at all and you will have to walk on the road itself. In this case, you must make sure you walk on the correct side of the road, so that you are facing the oncoming traffic.

Pedestrians are particularly at risk at junctions and crossings. The key things to remember as a pedestrian are:

- always cross the road at a designated pedestrian crossing, if possible. Make sure you follow the general rules regarding the use of crossings; for instance, do not start to cross a road if the 'green man' is already flashing.
- if you are crossing the road at a roundabout, treat this as a series of individual crossings and always look carefully to the left before stepping into the road. If the roundabout has a bridge or underpass, make sure you use this – do not be tempted to run across a busy highway just because it may be quicker.

### Key term

**Vulnerable road user** – an individual who is at an increased risk of being involved in an accident.

### Think about it

Think about what the phrase 'vulnerable road user' means. One definition is somebody who is at an increased risk of being involved in an accident.

- Find out how many motorcyclists are killed on the roads each year. What do you think this tells you? Are they a vulnerable road user?

- If you drive irresponsibly with friends in your car, there is nothing they can do about it. Does this make them vulnerable road users?

## Activity: Safer pedestrians

In 2007, 22 per cent of the people killed in road traffic accidents in Great Britain were pedestrians: 646 pedestrians were killed in road accidents in this year. This is a 78 per cent decrease from 1967, when 2964 pedestrians were killed in road accidents.

1. What changes do you think led to this reduction in the number of deaths of pedestrians?
2. What further improvements could be introduced to reduce the figures even more?

If you are walking at dusk, after dark or in **adverse weather conditions**, it is your responsibility to make yourself visible to other road users. You can do this by wearing a fluorescent, reflective tabard over your outer coat or jacket. It is a good idea to buy clothing which has been specifically designed to make you more visible to others; there is a wide range of such clothing available at reasonable prices, and it is always a good investment.

> **Key term**
>
> **Adverse weather conditions** – unfavourable weather conditions, such as high wind, heavy rain or snow.

## Elderly and disabled pedestrians, drivers and cyclists

All road users need to take particular care when they encounter elderly or disabled people on the roads. These people may not be able to react or move as quickly as other road users and you will need to show patience and tolerance. You will also need to adapt your driving or riding to ensure that you do not place them at risk.

Look out for signs highlighting places where the elderly may be crossing the road. Be aware that elderly riders or drivers may choose to travel more slowly than other road users, because they know that their reactions are no longer as quick as they were and they want to ensure their own safety as well as that of other road users.

## Child pedestrians and bicycle users

 Why are children vulnerable road users, particularly when travelling to and from school?

Many children use the roads and pavements every day to travel to and from school, to visit their friends, or to make their way to social activities. Some will choose to travel by bicycle, which places them at risk as road users. You will need to be aware of, and make allowances for, the fact that children do not always think and behave as you might expect. They may be excited or distracted by their friends, which could cause them to make poor choices. For instance, they might run out into the road, or forget to signal if they are turning right or left.

You will need to adapt your own behaviour when you encounter children on the roads. Take particular

care when you see them crossing the road, especially near schools and parks, and always make allowances for the unpredictable behaviour of children in groups. When children are excited and having fun, they are likely to forget to consider their road safety.

## Motorcycle and bicycle users

Users of motorcycles and bicycles are always vulnerable, because they are less visible than other road users. If you drive a car, you should take particular care to look out for motorcyclists and cyclists when pulling out from junctions or turning left. You also need to be aware that motorcycle and bicycle users are especially vulnerable when they are overtaking, or being overtaken by, other road users.

Motorcyclists and bicycle users have the additional problem that they need to negotiate road works and pot holes in the road. They will have to pull out to avoid these sorts of obstacle, so you need to be aware that this may happen and ready to adjust your direction as necessary.

## Horses

Horses are a common sight on the roads in many rural areas and you may also encounter them in towns and cities. Although the horse and rider may be well trained in road use, it is your responsibility to make allowances for them. Even the most well-trained horse may be unpredictable at times, especially if alarmed by a loud noise such as a car horn or the unexpected revving of an engine.

Give horse riders plenty of room and adjust your speed as you overtake. Always select an appropriate place and time to overtake and ensure that there is plenty of space to complete the manoeuvre. Never overtake on a bend where you cannot see the road ahead.

### Think about it

Before and after football matches, roads are usually congested with fans trying to get to and from their destination. The police often use horses to manage crowd behaviour.

Outline the procedure you would follow if you had to overtake a police horse on your motorcycle while the road was busy and crowded with football fans.

### Key safety information

- Always take care to adapt your driving when you see children or elderly pedestrians trying to cross the road.

- Take care when you encounter horses on the road: be aware that they may behave unpredictably.

- When pulling out at a junction, or turning left, look carefully for motorcycle or bicycle users.

### Just checking

1 Why do road users need to take particular care to look out for pedestrians at junctions and in poor weather conditions?
2 Explain why all road users need to give motorcyclists plenty of space when they are overtaking.
3 Why are children particularly vulnerable near schools and parks?

# Methods of traffic calming

Reducing vehicle speed saves lives

In this topic, you will learn about the different methods of traffic calming and their importance to the people who are trying to make our streets safer and more pleasant to live on. Traffic calming methods are used in residential areas to reduce the speed of traffic and are installed by the Highways Agency.

## Reasons for traffic calming

If you live on or near a busy road, you will be well aware of the problems caused by traffic. For example, the volume of traffic may make it difficult for you to cross the road, while the speed at which the traffic is travelling may make it difficult for you to try. Many roads in residential areas have not been designed to cope with large volumes of traffic, which makes accidents far more likely and puts vulnerable road users, such as young and elderly pedestrians, at particular risk.

People who live in residential areas often complain about the noise and air pollution from road vehicles. If residents feel that traffic calming methods are needed in their area, they should contact the local highways or road agency. These agencies will decide whether traffic calming is needed and, if so, which methods are most appropriate.

## Speed and survival rates for pedestrians in accidents

Recent research by the Department for Transport has shown that, if a pedestrian is hit by a car, their chances of survival are directly linked to the speed at which the car is travelling. One in five pedestrians hit by a car travelling at 30 miles per hour will die. However, if the car is travelling at 20 miles per hour, only one pedestrian in forty will die. A 1 per cent reduction in speed also reduces the likelihood of a crash by about 5 per cent. In response to this research, many areas have introduced 20 miles per hour speed limits near schools and in other areas with high rates of pedestrian injuries.

Reducing vehicle speed saves lives

# Types of traffic calming methods

| Traffic calming method | Main benefits |
|---|---|
| Road narrowing | Slows traffic down, reduces noise, reduces number of accidents, may encourage road users to seek alternative routes |
| **Chicanes** | Slow traffic down, reduce the risk of accidents. Usually used on more major roads |
| Bumpy road surface | Slows traffic down, reduces noise, reduces number of accidents, may encourage road users to seek alternative routes |
| Road humps/cushions | Slow traffic down, reduce noise levels, reduce number of accidents, may encourage road users to seek alternative routes |
| Raised pedestrian crossings | Slow traffic down, allow local residents to cross the road more safely, may reduce the number of accidents |
| Reduced speed limits | Slow traffic down, reduce noise levels, reduce the risk of accidents, reduce pollution levels, increase safety of local residents |
| Vehicle-activated speed warning signs | Slow traffic down, reduce noise levels, reduce the risk of accidents, reduce pollution, raise drivers'/riders' awareness of their speed |
| Road closures | Increase safety of pedestrians, especially children and the elderly. Make the local area quieter and reduce pollution levels |
| Mini roundabouts | Slow traffic down, reduce the number of accidents, allow local residents to cross the road more safely |

## Key term

**Chicane** – a man-made feature which creates extra turns in the road, in order to slow traffic down.

## Key safety information

- Slow down when approaching speed cushions or raised pedestrian crossings.

- Drive at an appropriate speed in residential areas, to ensure that you have enough time to stop if someone steps into the road in front of you.

- Contact the local highways or road agency if you feel that traffic calming is needed in the area in which you live. Your local council will have a contact number you can use.

## Activity: Local community road safety

Identify a residential area near to where you live that you feel would benefit from the introduction of road traffic calming methods.

1 Which specific issues cause problems for the people living in this area at the moment?

2 Which traffic calming measures would you introduce in this area and why?

## Just checking

1 Describe three methods of road calming commonly used in residential areas in the UK.

2 How effective is speed reduction in residential areas as a way of increasing the survival rates of pedestrians involved in road traffic accidents?

3 In what ways can traffic calming techniques improve the quality of life of people living in residential areas?

# The importance of correct signalling

In this topic, you will learn about the different forms of signalling used by road users and the possible dangers of miscommunication with other road users. You will develop your understanding of when and how to use particular types of signal such as your horn or lights. Different vehicles have a range of signalling methods which can be used to pass information to other road users.

Some of the information in this unit builds on the content in Unit 3 and is related to the signals used by the police and other road-crossing patrol personnel.

## Why signalling is important

As the driver or rider of a vehicle, it is your responsibility to signal your intentions to other road users so that they know what you are about to do. Correct signalling reduces the risk of misunderstandings and thus reduces the number of road traffic accidents. Always signal in plenty of time and continue to signal for long enough that other road users can see what you are intending to do. Ensure you cancel your signal after you have used it. Remember also that there are other clues to look for that may tell you that someone is about to turn, such as braking or their position on the road.

### When to signal

All road users need to signal when they move off from a stationary position. Remember to use the 'look (or 'mirror'), signal, **manoeuvre** routine to avoid possible accidents when pulling out into moving traffic. Use your indicators, or arm signals, to let other road users know if you are about to change your course (for instance, if you want to move from one lane to another) of if you intend to change direction.

### Using arm signals

Cyclists, motorcyclists, moped riders, horse riders and car users should all be familiar with the arm signals shown below. These signals are used to indicate changes in speed or direction, and users of motor vehicles will need to use these signals if their indicators or brake lights fail. Pedestrians should also understand what each signal means, so that they can react accordingly.

 Can you understand the indicator lights a car driver may use?

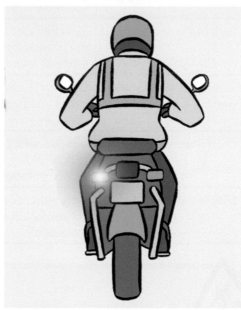 Can you understand the indicator lights a motorcyclist may use?

---

**Key term**

**Manoeuvre** – an action involving a change in course, often resulting in a change of direction.

Do you know what these arm signals mean?

## Activity: Signal practice time

Look carefully at the arm signals above. Working with a partner, practise using the signals and see whether your partner can understand what you are trying to show.

# When to use the horn or emergency lights and when to flash headlights

Riders and drivers of mopeds, motorcycles and cars can use a range of methods to pass on information or catch the attention of other road users. Your horn must only be used when your vehicle is moving, to warn other road users of your presence. You should not use your horn:

• when your vehicle is stationary

• in an aggressive manner

• in a built-up area between 11.30 pm and 7.00 am (because people will be sleeping).

However, this final rule may be broken if another road user is in danger.

**Emergency lights** – or hazard lights, as they are more commonly known – are used to let other road users know if you have a problem. You are likely to see them in use when a vehicle has broken down or if there is a hazard you need to be aware of such as a long queue of stationary traffic.

Road users may **flash their headlights** from low to high beam to show other road users that they are there. Some road users also flash their headlights to invite another driver to proceed with a manoeuvre. However, even if someone flashes their headlights at you, you should never carry out a manoeuvre unless you can see for yourself that it is safe to do so.

# Potential dangers related to signalling

As a road user, you must make sure that the signals you use are not confusing to others. Bicycle and horse riders are required to use hand signals and to ensure that these are clear. Signals must be given at the correct time so that other road users are able to interpret them and act accordingly and there is less risk of accidents occurring.

It is also important to avoid flashing your lights or sounding your horn in an aggressive manner, as this may intimidate other road users and may cause them to respond in an aggressive manner.

## Key terms

**Emergency lights** – lights used to indicate to other road users that there is a problem.

**Flash your headlights** – switch quickly between high beam and low beam lights; sometimes used by car drivers to pass on a message.

## Key safety information

- Always follow the sequence, 'look, signal, manoeuvre'.

- If your vehicle breaks down, remember to use your emergency lights to let other road users know that you have a problem.

- Never rely on the signals of other people. It is your responsibility to make sure that conditions are safe before you manoeuvre or change direction.

## Just checking

1  Identify the possible consequences of using your horn in an aggressive manner.
2  Why do all road users need to understand the hand signals used by cyclists and horse riders?
3  What signal would you expect to see if a car was slowing down but it had no working brake lights?

# Distractions to driving

In this topic, you will learn about the different types of distraction which can lead to accidents. All road users need to pay full attention at all times and make sure that they are not distracted by others. Passengers in or on any type of vehicle also need to make sure they do not distract the driver or rider.

People involved in road traffic accidents most commonly identify one of the following four factors as the cause of the accident:

- equipment failure
- road design
- poor road maintenance
- driver behaviour.

However, it is estimated that in more than 95 per cent of accidents, driver behaviour was the main cause, combined with one of the other factors above. Riders and drivers are likely to attribute accidents to other factors, since few people like to think that their own lack of attention led to an accident.

## Common causes of distraction

### Passenger behaviour

When you are riding or driving a vehicle, your passengers may be a significant distraction. For example, if you get involved in a conversation with your driver you will make it very difficult for them to focus fully on the road and they are more likely to be involved in an accident. Whenever you are in a vehicle – either as a driver or

⤵ What should you do if your passengers are making it difficult for you to concentrate on your driving?

as a passenger – it is important to avoid starting arguments or disagreements, since these are particularly likely to distract the driver. Similarly, conversations which may be upsetting should be saved for another time.

If you are the driver, passenger behaviour can also be distracting and it is important to deal with this in the right way. For instance, if you are being distracted by young children arguing in your vehicle, you should pull over before trying to resolve the issue. If you try to calm the situation while you are driving, you will not be able to focus on the road, and you will place yourself, your passengers and other road users at risk.

## Activity: Travelling home for Christmas

David is driving his mother and his two young children home to join his wife for Christmas. Tom is three years old, and Blossom is six months old. David's mother suffers from **dementia**. The journey will take about 90 minutes and is likely to be stressful for David.

- What sort of distractions is David likely to face?

### Key term

**Dementia** – a loss of mental capacity, more common in older people.

## Using a mobile phone

Most people carry a mobile phone with them, so that they can call for help if they break down or feel threatened. However, mobile phones are a significant distraction and should never be used while you are riding or driving a vehicle.

If you try to use your phone while riding or driving, you will have to take one hand off the steering wheel or handlebars and you will have to take your eyes off the road while dialling the number. Even hands-free systems usually require you to press at least one button. It has been shown that the reaction times of drivers using mobile telephones are 30 per cent slower than those of someone who is over the legal limit for alcohol. Texting is even more dangerous.

If you are caught using a mobile phone while driving, you could be fined up to £1000 and given three penalty points on your driving licence.

## Loud music

It is estimated that listening to loud music while trying to complete mental tasks or physical coordination activities may reduce your reaction times by up to 20 per cent compared to people completing the same tasks without listening to music. Music can also affect your moods. For instance, calming music may help you to relax, while lively music with a strong beat may make you more excited. Either mood could be hazardous to a rider or driver.

## Reading maps and using audio and navigational equipment

You should always plan your journey before you travel, not during your journey. Trying to read a map or program a satellite navigation system (satnav) while you are riding or driving is a major distraction and increases your risk of being involved in an accident. If you go off course or take a wrong turning, you should find a safe place to stop and pull off the road to re-plan your route.

## Eating and drinking

If you become hungry or thirsty while you are driving, it is important to pull off the road to have something to eat or drink. If you try to eat or drink while driving, you will have to take one hand off the steering wheel or handlebars, which will make it more difficult to direct your vehicle. You will also be less focused on your driving, which will increase the risks to yourself and to other road users.

## External distractions

It is important to remain focused as you travel. Try to avoid day dreaming, or becoming distracted by the countryside around you or by events taking place outside your vehicle. In particular, avoid slowing down to stare if you pass the scene of a road traffic accident, as this can lead to significant delays for the road users following you.

### Key safety information

- Always pull off the road if your passengers are distracting you. Do not try to deal with them as you ride or drive.

- Do not use your mobile phone while you are driving or riding your vehicle.

- Plan your journey before you set off. Do not try to read a map or set your satellite navigation system while you are driving.

### Just checking

1 Identify three possible consequences of trying to drink a bottle of soft drink while riding a bicycle or motorcycle.

2 Why do motor vehicle passengers need to be aware of their own behaviour, even though they are not driving?

3 Explain how music can be a distraction from good driving.

# Showing consideration for other road users

In this topic, you will learn about the importance of showing consideration to other road users. Being a good driver involves more than simply knowing the rules of the road: you also need to consider and care about the other road users. If all road users did this, the roads would be much safer and many accidents could be avoided.

### Key terms

**Courtesy** – consideration of and respect for others.

**Patience** – tolerance in difficult situations (e.g. traffic jams).

## Respecting the rights of all road users

What precautions should you take if you need to overtake a horse and rider?

### Showing courtesy and patience

It is important to be courteous to other road users at all times, as this will make the roads safer and more pleasant for everyone. Be polite to other road users; for example, thank someone if they let you out at a junction.

Be aware of vulnerable road users and treat them with respect. For instance, if you encounter a horse and rider on the roads, consider their safety, give them plenty of space and do not 'rev' your engine or try to overtake if it is unsafe to do so. You will gain nothing by behaving in an inconsiderate manner and if the horse becomes distressed, you may cause an accident.

It is also important to be patient, since impatience may increase your chances of being involved in an accident and driving more quickly often gains you little in terms of time. Avoid risky overtaking and never take unnecessary risks just to try to save a little time.

## Activity: How much time do I gain?

People often believe that riding or driving a little more quickly will make a big difference to their journey time. However, this is not the case. The real issue is that the road conditions often dictate the speed at which you can complete a journey. Trying to drive fast does not result in a much increased average speed but it can increase your risk of having an accident.

1 What effect will speeding have on your braking? Are you likely to brake more or less?
2 What effect will speeding have on how much fuel you use? Is it more expensive or less?

# Signalling intentions to others

You should always signal your intentions to other road users. This is especially important for motorcycle, moped and bicycle users, who need to do everything they can to make themselves more noticeable to other road users.

Many people forget to signal, or simply do not consider the people around them. You should try to remain alert at all times, so that you are ready to respond to the actions of other road users. This will reduce your chances of being involved in an accident.

# Keeping safe distances from other road users

Many people drive or ride too close to the vehicle in front of them. This is dangerous for two reasons: firstly, if the vehicle in front has to brake suddenly, it is likely that the driver behind will not be able to react in time and there will be a collision. Secondly, many road users find it very stressful to have someone following close behind them, and this could cause them to make poor decisions, which may lead to an accident. For these reasons, you should always leave a safe distance between your own vehicle and the vehicle in front of you and give other road users the space they need. If somebody overtakes you and pulls in directly in front of you, brake slowly and recreate the necessary space between the vehicles.

If you are one of several cyclists or motorcyclists riding together, avoid riding as a 'pack', since this will make it difficult for others to overtake you safely.

## Using dipped headlights

If an approaching road user does not dip their headlights, the glare may dazzle you. If you cannot see clearly, you are more likely to be involved in an accident. Therefore, it is important to dip your headlights whenever you approach another road user, as a matter of courtesy. This is true whether you are approaching a motor vehicle, a bicycle, a horse or a pedestrian – all road users will face the same problems if they cannot see.

# Consideration of vulnerable road users

## The importance of giving way to emergency vehicles and buses

If you see or hear the flashing lights or sirens of an emergency vehicle, you should always pull over and stop so that the vehicle can pass you (as long as it is safe to do so). If you are at a roundabout or a junction, remember that emergency

**Think about it**

**Up close and personal**

The recommended distances between vehicles depend on various conditions.

Find a copy of the Highway Code and research the 'safe distances' you should allow if you are in a car or riding a moped:

- at 70 miles per hour
- at 30 miles per hour
- on wet roads
- on icy roads.

How can poor parking be a hazard for different road users?

vehicles always have priority and they may cross red traffic lights (although you do not have the right to do so if you are moving out of their way). It is usually safest simply to wait until the emergency vehicle has passed before continuing with your journey. Be aware that any delay could be the difference between life and death for the person or people the emergency vehicle is trying to reach.

You should give way to buses if it is safe to do so, especially when they are trying to pull out of a bus stop. This is important because buses are large and therefore more difficult to turn and manoeuvre. You also need to remember that the bus driver may not be able to see you in their mirrors, especially if you are on a motorcycle or bicycle.

## Parking

Never park where you will be causing an obstruction or endangering other road users. Look carefully for parking restrictions (often indicated by single or double yellow lines) and avoid parking in a restricted zone. These restrictions are intended to protect other road users and ease the flow of traffic and if you ignore them, you could be issued with a parking ticket or fine or your vehicle could be removed.

When parking, make sure you do not block in other vehicles. This sort of thoughtless behaviour is a major cause of frustration for road users and your own vehicle may also be at risk if the person you have blocked in is determined to remove their vehicle despite the risk of damage. Practise your parking skills so that you can ensure your vehicle is always parked straight and no part of the vehicle is outside the parking zone if there is one indicated.

 Why is it important to obey all road markings?

## Consideration of pedestrians

Pedestrians – especially young children, older people and disabled people – are among the most vulnerable people on the roads. It is important to be aware of the difficulties pedestrians may face; for example, elderly people may need more time to cross the road, people who are deaf or hard of hearing may not hear your vehicle approaching, and people who are blind or partially sighted will need to be treated with particular care.

You will also need to take care if the pavements are closed (for example, due to road works) or absent. If pedestrians have to walk on the road itself, you must give them plenty of space and avoid overtaking until it is safe to do so.

## Obeying the rules of the road

As a road user, you must obey all road signs, road markings and traffic lights, including temporary lights or signals. Following the basic rules of the road will allow traffic to flow freely and should increase the safety of all road users. You should always consider the rights and needs of other road users and never break the rules of the road simply because you think it might save you some time.

When travelling on the motorway, remain in the left-hand lane unless overtaking other vehicles. People who spend their entire journey in the middle lane force other drivers to move into the outside lane if they wish to overtake, which can be frustrating and potentially dangerous.

**Key safety information**

- Always drive with dipped headlights.

- Show patience and consideration for all road users and treat them as you would expect to be treated yourself.

- When parking, take care that you do not block in other road users.

**Just checking**

1   What are the possible consequences of going through a set of red traffic lights in your rush to get to work on time?

2   What are the possible consequences of driving too close to other vehicles in the outside lane of a motorway?

3   Why do you think so many people do not signal their intentions to other road users? Discuss your ideas with a friend.

# Actions which cause conflict

In this topic, you will learn about the different ways in which your actions can lead to a negative response from other road users. Aggressive riding and driving are common and around 1500 people in the UK are injured or killed each year as a result of disputes between road users. You need to make sure that you are not one of these people.

## Failing to show consideration for other road users

### Inattention to the road

Many accidents, or near accidents, are caused by simple errors such as not checking mirrors before manoeuvring, so you need to make sure that you are focused on your riding or driving at all times. For example, if you are driving a car, make sure that your mirrors are appropriately positioned before you set off and be aware of any **blind spot** in your view of the road around you. It is particularly important to focus when you see other traffic joining a road or filtering in on a motorway.

### Ignoring the rules of the road

If you ignore the basic rules of the road, you are likely to encounter negative responses from other road users. For instance, if you break the speed limit, you will endanger yourself and other road users. Similarly, if you weave in and out of traffic and **cut up** other drivers, you are likely to irritate the road users around you and you may cause an accident.

Always obey traffic signs and signals and avoid behaving in an inconsiderate or aggressive manner. This should help to prevent conflict with other road users, which in turn should reduce your risk of being involved in an accident or other incident.

 What precautions should you take if you need to overtake a cyclist?

### Key terms

**Cut up** – pull in ahead of another vehicle without warning, forcing them to brake sharply or swerve to avoid you.

**Blind spot** – an area that the rider or driver of a vehicle cannot see through their front windscreen or in their mirrors.

# Aggressive behaviour

## Tailgating

If someone drives or rides too close to the back of your vehicle (closer than the two-second distance recommended by the Highway Code), they are **tailgating** you. Tailgating increases the risk of an accident, since the driver or rider behind will not be able to stop in time if the vehicle in front brakes sharply and their visibility may be reduced if they are following a large vehicle such as a bus or lorry.

Drivers who are tailgated are likely to feel stressed and pressurised, which may cause them to break the speed limit or make mistakes in their driving. These factors also increase the chances of accidents. You must make sure that you do not tailgate other vehicles and if you are being tailgated yourself, remain calm and try to allow the vehicle behind to overtake you if possible. Do not speed up, as the vehicle behind is likely to speed up as well and you will endanger yourself and other road users.

## Inappropriate use of the horn and using gestures

If you are impolite or aggressive towards other road users, you may provoke a similar response, which could lead to a confrontation. In order to avoid upsetting other road users, it is important not to sound your horn repeatedly or make rude gestures. Even if someone does not hear or see exactly what you say or do, they will be able to see that you are being rude.

## Showing irritation to others

A simple action or gesture – such as rolling your eyes as you pass another vehicle – may provoke an angry response. Make sure you treat other road users with respect at all times and remember that it is best to mind your own business and avoid conflict wherever possible.

## Competitive riding and driving

An increasing number of road accidents and deaths are caused by young people racing their friends on the roads. This sort of behaviour is often unplanned and may simply be due to high spirits. It is important not to become involved in such activity, even if you are encouraged by your friends or peers: the roads are not designed for racing and you will place yourself and those around you at risk. This type of behaviour is also likely to provoke a negative response from other road users.

**Key term**

**Tailgating** – following another vehicle too closely.

### Over-cautious behaviour

It can be extremely frustrating to encounter someone who is riding or driving slowly or in an over-cautious way (for instance, a new driver, an elderly person, or someone who is not sure where they are going). It is difficult to know why the person is driving so cautiously or to predict how they are likely to behave. In these circumstances, it is important not to respond in an aggressive way. If you follow the vehicle too closely, you are likely to put the driver under pressure and you will not have time to respond if they need to brake sharply. Be patient and do not overtake until you are sure that it is safe to do so.

If you have just passed your test and are still building up your confidence, you can display a 'P' plate on your vehicle. This will let other road users know what to expect.

**Key safety information**

- Never make obscene or rude gestures at other road users, however angry or frustrated you are.

- Follow accepted procedures at junctions and traffic lights.

- Never attempt to race another road user.

## Activity: How would you react?

Explain how you would you respond in each of the following situations.

1 You are being tailgated by another vehicle.
2 The driver in front of you is driving at 25 miles per hour in a 40 miles per hour zone.
3 You are overtaken by a car with a group of youths in it; the youths are shouting at you and making obscene gestures.

### Just checking

1 Describe two actions taken by car drivers that are likely to provoke a negative response from motorcyclists or scooter riders.

2 Why is it important to be patient when you encounter slow riders or drivers on the roads?

3 How would you feel if another vehicle cut in in front of you after you had been queuing patiently for 30 minutes, waiting to exit a motorway? How should you respond in this situation?

# Managing conflict

In this topic, you will learn how to respond to and manage conflict situations that you may encounter as a road user. These situations may arise due to an error or fault on your part, or they may result from the actions of another road user. It is important to respond calmly and responsibly, so that conflicts are resolved effectively.

## Recognising unsafe driver behaviour

As a passenger, you need to be aware if the rider or driver you are with is not concentrating or is behaving in an unsafe manner. If such behaviour continues, all road users will be at risk. If you are the cause of, or are contributing to, the problem, you will need to change your behaviour. For example, if an argument has developed between the people in a car, it is best to stop the conversation until the journey has finished or to pull over. If the rider or driver has been distracted by events outside the vehicle, you should remind them to focus on their driving.

Many accidents and deaths on the roads could be avoided if riders and drivers were more aware of their own behaviour.

## Being tolerant of others errors, poor attitudes and behaviour

Remember that everyone makes mistakes and try to avoid conflict if you can. If you are in the wrong, acknowledge your mistake and apologise – either in words or by putting your hand up to show another road user that you realise you have made a mistake.

 Getting angry or aggressive won't help to solve this problem

If someone apologises to you, accept their apology and drop the issue: there is nothing to be gained in continuing an argument needlessly. Be aware that some people are not as considerate as they should be in their attitudes and behaviour and try to be **tolerant** of other road users.

## Staying calm when faced with aggressive riders and drivers

If you encounter a road user who seems determined to start an argument – whether or not they have any reason to do so – you must remain calm and avoid being drawn into a dispute. If the other road user is behaving in an aggressive manner, remain in your vehicle with the windows wound up and the doors locked. If you feel threatened, try to move away from the situation as soon as you can. If you feel that you have been intimidated by the other road user (or road users), note down the driver's or rider's vehicle registration number and report this to the police.

> ### Key terms
>
> **Tolerant** – accepting of others and their behaviour, even if it is unfamiliar and unexpected.
>
> **Defusing tension** – making a situation less dangerous, tense or hostile.

## Activity: What to do if you are followed by an aggressive road user

What should you do if, having left the scene of a confrontation, you are followed by the other road user? Which of the following solutions would be most appropriate?

1  Drive on, rather than stopping.
2  Drive to a police station or look for a police officer.
3  Avoid quiet areas and head for a busy, crowded location.
4  Drive to a busy shopping centre car park, stop and sound your horn repeatedly.

## Defusing tension

In order to reduce the tension during a disagreement or dispute with another road user, you should try to use some or all of the following techniques.

| Technique | Action involved |
|---|---|
| Acknowledge the problem | Discuss with the other person what has happened and what the problem is |
| Remain calm | Try to avoid making the situation worse through your actions or behaviour |
| Ask open questions | Ask questions which will enable the other person to explain to you, from their own viewpoint, what has happened |
| Confirm understanding | At the end of the discussion, check with the other person that you both understand what has been said |
| Agree action | Before you leave, decide together what should happen next (e.g. you both need to contact your insurance companies) |

## Seeking advice and training

If you have been involved in an accident or dispute, you may wish to seek professional advice about how to handle any problems which arise. You could contact your insurance company if there has been damage to your vehicle, or if you have damaged another vehicle. If you have been injured or seriously distressed by an incident, you may need to go to hospital or visit your GP, or seek counselling.

If you have experienced road rage from a road user, you may wish to report this to the police so that they can investigate the case. It may give you a sense of closure and help you to recover from the incident and – if the road user is caught – you will also be doing other road users a favour.

## How to handle tailgating and impatience

As a road user, you will almost certainly find yourself being followed too closely by another rider or driver. This may be because the road user behind you is travelling more

 Driving too close to other vehicles can cause anxiety for the driver

quickly than you are; if this is the case, you should let them overtake if possible. Ensure you leave space in front of your vehicle so that they can overtake and if you are on a dual carriageway or motorway, try to move into an inner lane.

If, however, the rider or driver behind you is deliberately driving too close, in an aggressive manner, you may choose to turn off the road or go around a roundabout a second time, in order to try to lose them. This will add only a few minutes to your journey and will allow you to avoid the stress and conflict that tailgating can cause. If you feel distressed or threatened, you may wish to take a short break to allow yourself to recover.

## Recovering from confrontations

If you have been involved in a dispute or conflict, or if you have been frightened or distressed by another road user's behaviour, you will need to regain your composure before you carry on riding or driving. If you are driving or riding a vehicle, you may wish to pull over in a safe spot and take a few minutes to gather yourself before you move on. These sorts of action are important because you may have a delayed reaction to the incident and you will put other road users at risk if you carry on when you are not safe to drive.

If you feel that you have lost confidence after an accident or incident, you may wish to book additional training with a riding or driving school. The instructors will work with you to regain and improve your skills and to help you to regain your confidence.

## Awareness of cultural differences

The UK is a multicultural society, and many road users have learned to ride or drive in another country with different rules and expectations. These people may behave in a way you do not expect and their actions and behaviours may not have the meanings you expect. It is particularly important to be aware of these differences when interpreting signals given to you by other road users.

> **Did you know?**
>
> In the UK, repeated use of the horn is usually interpreted as a sign of aggression, or a request for help or support. It is important to be aware of the different ways in which signals may be interpreted. In China and many other countries, drivers use the horn to let others know that they are coming through, and repeated sounding of the horn is not seen as aggressive.

## Activity: Calm down, calm down!

Imagine you have just had a confrontation with another road user at a roundabout. The other road user was verbally aggressive to you and you are extremely angry and upset.

1 How will you deal with this situation immediately after the confrontation?

2 What actions (if any) might you take later on, when you have regained your composure?

### Key safety information

- Never tailgate another vehicle. If you find that you are too close, drop back to allow a safe stopping distance.

- If you are upset by an incident on the road, pull over and allow yourself time to regain your composure.

- If you encounter an aggressive road user, note down their vehicle registration number and report them to the police.

### Just checking

1 What can you do to calm a situation if you have been the cause of a dispute?

2 Why is it dangerous to flash your lights repeatedly at the vehicle in front if you want the driver or rider to move over?

3 How could you, as a passenger, help the rider or driver you are with if they have been upset by a road rage incident?

# Assessment overview

While working through this unit, you will have prepared for the following assessment tasks:

| 1.1 | Identify types of vulnerable road users | Pages 77–79 |
|-----|-----------------------------------------|-------------|
| 2.1 | Suggest traffic calming measures that could be used in a specified area | Pages 80–81 |
| 3.1 | Identify examples of effective and ineffective signalling by road users | Pages 82–84 |
| 3.2 | Identify common distractions that can contribute to accidents | Pages 85–87 |
| 3.3 | Describe ways in which consideration can be shown for other road users | Pages 88–91 |
| 3.4 | Identify behaviour which can lead to negative responses in others | Pages 92–94 |
| 3.5 | Describe ways of managing behaviour when dealing with other road users | Pages 95–99 |

edexcel
advancing learning, changing lives

# Assignment tips

This unit is meant to be a very practical unit in which you will explore your local road network, develop your knowledge of the risks for road users in these areas and suggest ways in which these risks could be reduced or avoided.

➋ **Task 1.** To meet the assessment criteria, you will need to identify vulnerable road users in terms of:

- types of people (e.g. children, teenagers)
- modes of transport (e.g. bicycle riders, motorcyclists).

You will need to explain what makes each group of people vulnerable and you may be able to combine this task with your research for Task 2.

➋ **Task 2.** To meet the assessment criteria, you will need to select a network of roads in your local area which do not currently have traffic calming methods and suggest appropriate traffic calming methods that could be introduced. Your evidence is likely to be in the form of self-drawn maps which show the changes you are proposing.

➋ **Task 3.** To meet the assessment criteria, you will need to consider the attitudes and behaviours of road users. You could gather evidence by:

- observing road users in a variety of locations
- travelling as a passenger on public or private transport
- taking video footage of road users in your area.

You could present your evidence in the form of:

- a log
- short written descriptions
- annotated maps with descriptions, diagrams and pictures to add depth and show what actually happened.

# Index

A roads  11
accidents  41–2
   distractions leading to  85–7
   first aid  46–7
   legal requirements  43–5
   seeking advice  97
   survival rates of pedestrians  80
advanced stop lines  60
adverse weather conditions  78
age of road users  13
aggressive road users  92–4, 96, 98
alcohol  14–15
animals  39, 45, 66
antifreeze  27
aquaplaning  20
arm signals  68–9
attentive drivers/riders  85, 92

B roads  11
bicycles
   checks and maintenance  32–3
   *see also* cyclists/cycling
black ice  20
bleeding  47
blind spot  92
blow-out  25
brake fluid  27, 29
brakes
   bicycles  32
   motorbikes/mopeds  29
breakdowns  38–9
   at level crossings  72–3
breaks  8, 9
bridle  35
burns  47
buses, giving way to  90

cars
   checks and maintenance  25–8
   financial costs  6–7
cats, running over  45
chain
   bicycle  32
   motorcycle  29

chicanes  81
children
   distracting the driver  85
   and the Green Cross Code  52
   helmet for horse riding  34–5, 61
   school crossing patrols  65
   vulnerability of  78–9, 91
clothing
   cyclists  33, 56
   horse riders  34
   motorcyclists  31
   pedestrians  51, 78
$CO_2$ emissions  25
comfort breaks  8, 9
competitive driving  93
conflict
   actions causing  92–4
   managing  95–9
confrontations, recovering from  98
consideration of other road users  88–91
controlled drugs  14, 15–16
controlled level crossings  71–2
costs and benefits, transport  3–5
costs of private vehicle use  6–7
courtesy  88
crossing roads safely
   cyclists  58
   pedestrians  51–5, 77
cultural differences  98
'cutting up' of other drivers/riders  92
cycling helmet  33
cyclists/cycling
   accident outcomes  12
   advanced stop lines  60
   clothing  33, 56
   crossing roads  58
   fines, drink drive limit  15
   Highway Code  56–8
   night journeys  21
   road junctions  57–8
   vulnerability of  79
   and weather conditions  20–1
   *see also* bicycles

darkness, dangers of 21
daylight running lights 30
defusing tension 96
dementia 86
dipped headlights, use of 89
disabled drivers 40
disabled pedestrians 78
disposal costs 6, 7
distance from other road users 89
distractions 18, 85–7
dogs, running over 45
DRABC mnemonic 47
drinking
    alcohol, effect on driving 14–15
    while driving, distraction of 87
driving licence, graduated 19
drugs 14–15
duty of care 43

eating while driving 87
elderly road users 78
emergency care, providing 47
emergency lights 83, 84
emergency services, contacting 42
emergency telephones 39–40
emergency vehicles, giving way to 55, 70, 89–90
emotions, effect on performance 18
energy sources 5
environmental costs 5
exhaust, motorcycle 31

fatigue 17–18
fines
    cycling when over drink drive limit 15
    mobile phone use 86
first aid 46–7
flashing of headlights 83, 84
flashing red lights 69–70
fluid levels, checking 36
fluorescent clothing 56
fluorescent tail guard 61
fog 20
fuel costs 7
fuel leakage 41
fuel types 5

gender of road users 13
gestures, use of 93
graduated driving licences 19
Green Cross Code 52
grid system, maps 10

handbooks 37
hazard warning lights 38, 84
headlights
    dipping 89
    flashing 83, 84
helmets
    cyclists 33
    horse riders 34–5, 61
    motorcyclists 31, 59
Highway Code
    cyclists 56–8
    horse riders 61–2
    level crossings 71–3
    motorcyclists 59–60
    obeying 92
    pedestrians 51–5
    traffic lights 68–70
    traffic signs 63–7
    tramways 73
Highways Agency 39–40
horn, use of 83–4, 93, 98
horse riding
    checks 34–5
    Highway Code 61–2
horse shoes 35
horses, overtaking 79, 88
hot weather 60
hybrid cars 5
hypnotic effects of driving 18

ice on roads 20
impatient drivers 96–7
inattentive drivers/riders 92
indicator lights 26, 30
    using during signalling 82
initial costs 6
instruction signs 64
insurance company, reporting accidents to 44
insurance costs 7
Internet guides 37

journey planning 8–9
junctions
   advanced stop lines at 60
   cyclists negotiating 57–8
   pedestrians at risk 77

legal requirements, accidents 43–4
level crossings 71–3
   flashing red lights 69–70
lights, checking 26, 30, 33
lubricant 29, 30

maintenance
   bicycles 32–3
   cars 25–8
   motorcycles 29–31
maps 10
   reading while driving 87
mobile phone use 86
mopeds see motorcycles/motorcyclists
motorcycles/motorcyclists
   accident outcomes 12
   carrying passengers 59
   checks and maintenance 29–31
   financial costs 7
   helmets 31, 59
   risk taking 9
   vulnerability of 79
   and weather conditions 21–2, 60
motorways 10–11
   breakdowns 38, 39–40
   considerate driving 91
MOTs 43
music, distraction of 86

night journeys 21
non-renewable resources 5
non-toxic substances 47

oil levels, checking 27
open level crossings 72
over-cautious behaviour 94
overtaking
   cyclists 79, 92
   horses 79, 88
   on the motorway 91
   pedestrians 91
   slow drivers 94

parking 90–1
passenger behaviour 85–6
patience 88
pavement 51
pedestrians
   consideration of 91
   crossing the road safely 52, 54
   high visibility clothing 51
   safety guidance rules 51–5
   vulnerability of 77–9
peer group 13
performance of road users, factors impairing
   14–21
physical health, effect on road use 14
planning a journey 8–9
police, reporting accidents to 44
prescription drugs 14, 15–16
primary routes 11
private vehicles, costs of using 6–7
professional advice 37
psychological states of mind 17–19

racing 93
radiator coolant 27
railway level crossings 69–73
rain 20
reaction time 15
reflective clothing/accessories 56
reflective fetlock bands, horses 61
reflective tail guard, horses 61
reflector on bicycles 33
relaxation breaks 8, 9
respect, showing 88–91
risk taking 9, 88
road maps 10
road rage 97
road signs 10–11, 63–7
road types 12
roundabouts
   horse riders crossing 62
   pedestrians crossing 77
   traffic calming (mini) 81
route planning 9

rules *see* Highway Code
running a car, costs of  6

safe distance, keeping  89
safety checks  36–7
school crossing patrols  65
scooters *see* motorcycles/motorcyclists
servicing costs  7
shock, symptoms of  46–7
signalling  68–9, 82–4, 89
snow  20
social costs of road use  5
speed limits  13, 80
suspension, motorcycle  30

tabards  21, 39
tack, horses  35
tailgating  93, 97–8
taxation  7
tension, defusing  96
time of day  13
tiredness  17–18
tolerance  95–6
toucan crossings  58
traction  35
traffic accidents  5
traffic calming methods  80–1
traffic light signals  69

emergency services  70
level crossings  69–70
traffic signs
giving instructions  64
giving orders  63
giving warnings  66–7
school crossing patrols  65
tramways  71, 73
tunnel vision  9
tyre pressures  25–6, 29

unsafe driver behaviour, recognising  95

vehicle safety checks  36–7
visibility  20, 30, 41
vulnerable road users  77–9

walking  51, 78
*see also* pedestrians
warning signs  66–7
warning triangles  39
water coolant  27
weather conditions  20–1, 78
windscreen chips/cracks  28
windscreen fluid  27
windscreen wipers  28
windy weather  20–1, 60